MY SENIOR TRIP

1943-1945 Camp White to Japan Letters Home

CD Griffith

ARCHWAY
PUBLISHING

Archway Publishing books may be ordered through booksellers or by contacting:

Archway Publishing
1663 Liberty Drive
Bloomington, IN 47403
www.archwaypublishing.com
844-669-3957

ISBN: 978-1-6657-1282-8 (sc)
ISBN: 978-1-6657-1283-5 (e)

Library of Congress Control Number: 2021919657

Print information available on the last page.

Archway Publishing rev. date: 11/18/2021

INTRODUCTION

C.D. Griffith was drafted his senior year of high school in Coalmont Indiana. He entered the army on March 2, 1943 one month prior to his high school graduation day.

He lived on his family farm in the Eel River bottoms where he worked on the farm, hunted and fished his early years and was never more than 25 miles from home. In March of 1943, with a brief stop at Fort Benjamin Harrison in Indianapolis he was on a train to Camp White in Medford Oregon with a final stop in Japan.

This book is a collection of original letters written home to his family. They contain errors in spelling and structure however they are the thoughts of an 18-year-old young man and a lot of history.

Jeffrey D Griffith

The folks he wrote to and about:

Mom and Dad

Pud (his brother Gary)

Jackie (his sister Jack)

Terry (his nephew)

Bugs (his brother in law)

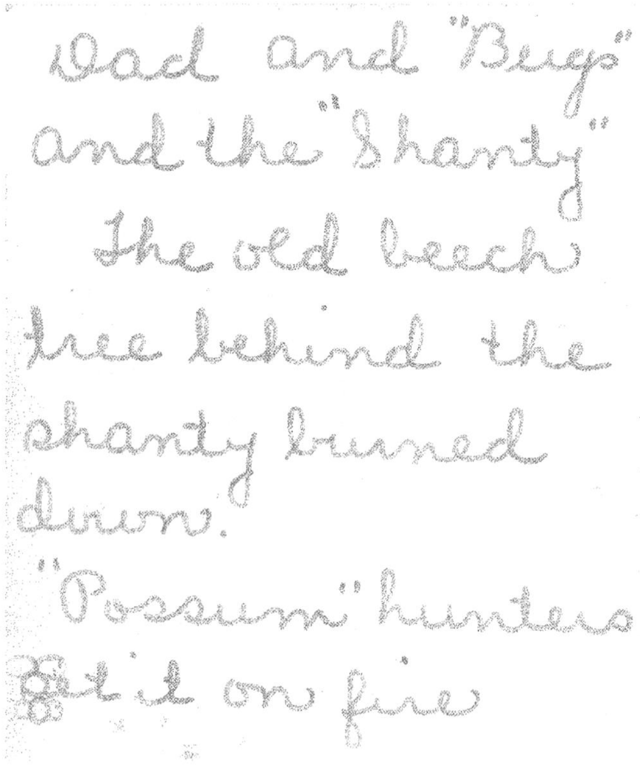
Dad and "Bugs"
and the "Shanty"
The old beech
tree behind the
shanty burned
down.
"Possum" hunters
set it on fire

Mickie – friend no photo
Norma – friend no photo
Ruby – friend no photo

Dec. '42

48 Gratcham St.
Hammond, Indiana

App. not Req.

Prepare in Duplicate

Local Board No. 1 51
Clay County 021
FEB 19 1943 001
12½ W. National Ave.
Brazil, Indiana

(Local Board Date Stamp With Code)

Feb. 19, 1943
(Date of mailing)

ORDER TO REPORT FOR INDUCTION

The President of the United States,

To Courtney (First name) Dale (Middle name) Griffith (Last name)

Order No. 11,937

GREETING:

Having submitted yourself to a local board composed of your neighbors for the purpose of determining your availability for training and service in the land or naval forces of the United States, you are hereby notified that you have now been selected for training and service therein.

You will, therefore, report to the local board named above at American Legion Hall, Brazil, Ind. (Place of reporting)

at 7:15 (Hour of reporting) a. m., on the 2nd day of March, 1943

This local board will furnish transportation to an induction station. You will there be examined, and, if accepted for training and service, you will then be inducted into the land or naval forces.

Persons reporting to the induction station in some instances may be rejected for physical or other reasons. It is well to keep this in mind in arranging your affairs, to prevent any undue hardship if you are rejected at the induction station. If you are employed, you should advise your employer of this notice and of the possibility that you may not be accepted at the induction station. Your employer can then be prepared to replace you if you are accepted, or to continue your employment if you are rejected.

Willful failure to report promptly to this local board at the hour and on the day named in this notice is a violation of the Selective Training and Service Act of 1940, as amended, and subjects the violator to fine and imprisonment.

If you are so far removed from your own local board that reporting in compliance with this order will be a serious hardship and you desire to report to a local board in the area of which you are now located, go immediately to that local board and make written request for transfer of your delivery for induction, taking this order with you.

Harry C. Hyatt
Member or clerk of the local board.

U. S. GOVERNMENT PRINTING OFFICE 16—18271-5

D. S. S. Form 150
(Revised 1-15-43)

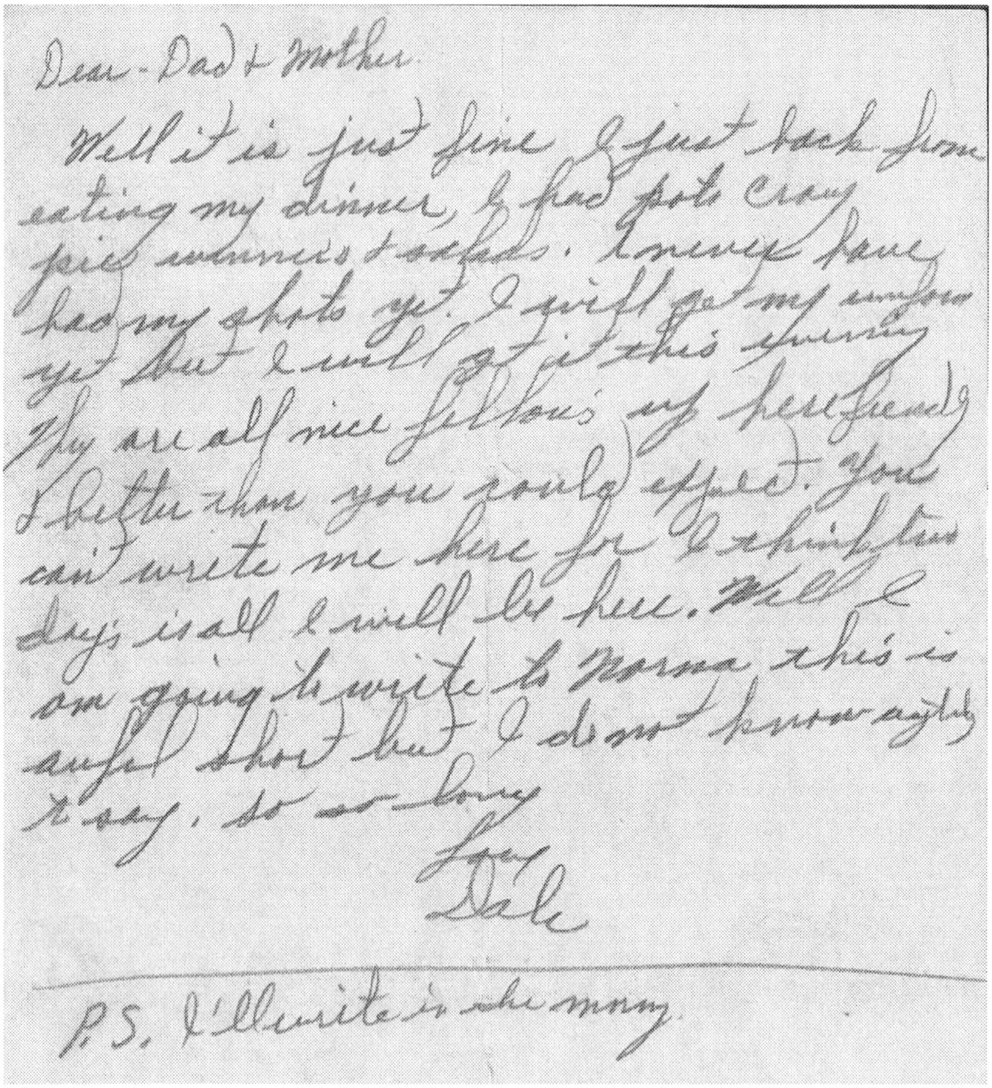

Dear- Dad + mother.

Well it is just fine I just back from eating my dinner, I had poto cray pie weiners + salads. I never have had my shots yet. I will get my uniform yet but I will get it this evening They are all nice fellows up here friendly + better than you could expect. You can't write me here for I think two day's is all I will be here. Well I am going to write to Norma this is awful short but I don't know anything to say, so so long

Love
Dale

P.S. I'll write in the morning.

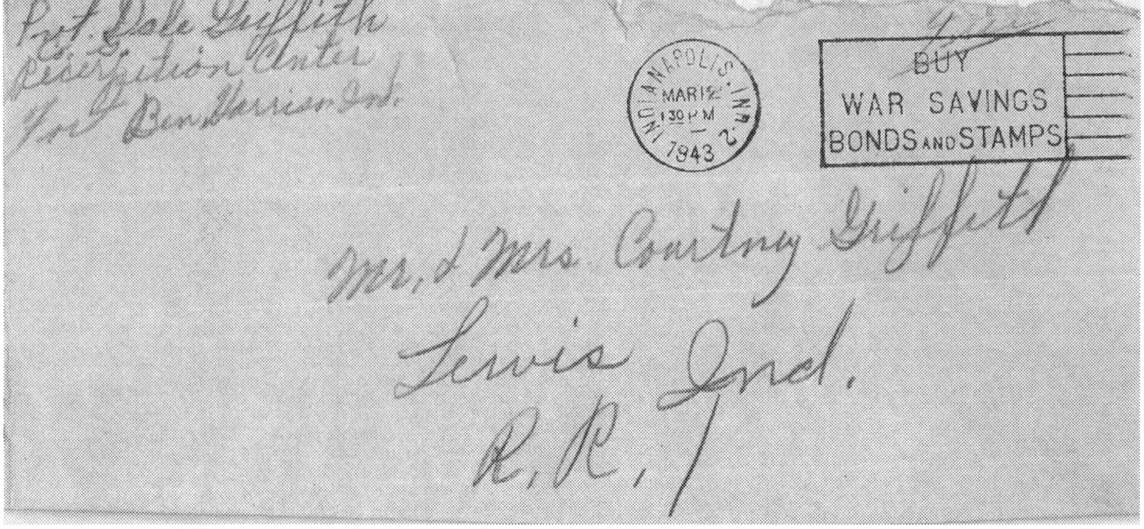

Pvt. Dale Griffith
Co. G.
Reception Center
Fort Ben Harrison Ind.

Mr. & Mrs. Courtny Griffith
Lewis Ind.
R.R. 1

THE UNITED STATES OF AMERICA

VETERANS' ADMINISTRATION

WASHINGTON, D. C.

National Service Life Insurance

DATE INSURANCE EFFECTIVE MARCH 10, 1943

CERTIFICATE NO. N- 5 310 177

This Certifies That COURTNEY D. GRIFFITH

has applied for insurance in the amount of $ 10,000., payable in case of death.

Subject to the payment of the premiums required, this insurance is granted under the authority of The National Service Life Insurance Act of 1940, and subject in all respects to the provisions of such Act, of any amendments thereto, and of all regulations thereunder, now in force or hereafter adopted, all of which, together with the application for this insurance, and the terms and conditions published under authority of the Act, shall constitute the contract.

VETERANS ADMINISTRATION

Administrator of Veterans' Affairs.

Countersigned at Washington, D. C.

APR 1 1943
(Date)

Registrar.

Mr. Courtney Lee Griffith
RR 1
Lewis, Ind.

Insurance Form 360

IMPORTANT NOTICE

This certificate is issued as evidence that National Service Life Insurance, in the amount specified, has been granted the individual named, subject to the provisions of The National Service Life Insurance Act of 1940, and subsequent amendments. If the person to whom this certificate is sent is other than the individual named therein, it is sent to you for safekeeping in accordance with directions contained in the application and you should notify the insured of receipt.

This insurance, or part of it in multiples of $500 (but not less than $1,000), may be converted at any time after it has been in force 1 year and within 5 years from the effective date, to a policy of insurance on the Ordinary Life, 20-Payment Life, or 30-Payment Life plans.

Unless changed to another plan of insurance, this insurance will terminate at the expiration of the 5-year period.

The insured may change the beneficiary without the consent of the previous beneficiary named. This insurance is not assignable and is not subject to the claims of creditors.

Should a claim arise under this insurance, it should be directed to the Veterans' Administration, Washington, D. C., in order to secure a prompt settlement. It will not be necessary to consult or employ an attorney, claim agent, or other person to secure benefits under this insurance, but if one is consulted or employed, the law prohibits the payment of any fee except as allowed by the Veterans' Administration or by a court in a judgment on the policy. (See Secs. 616 and 617, National Service Life Insurance Act of 1940.)

Always give the certificate number when corresponding with the Veterans' Administration regarding this insurance.

16—18128-1 ☆ U. S. GOVERNMENT PRINTING OFFICE : 1941

VETERANS ADMINISTRATION
Insurance Form 350
Rev. Sept. 1942

APPLICATION FOR NATIONAL SERVICE LIFE INSURANCE

UNDER SECTION 602 (a) NATIONAL SERVICE LIFE INSURANCE ACT OF 1940 AS AMENDED AND REGULATIONS OF THE VETERANS ADMINISTRATION WITHOUT REPORT OF PHYSICAL EXAMINATION

For use by persons in the active service in the land or naval forces of the United States within 120 days after the date of entrance into the active service. NOTE.—Persons in the active service more than 120 days and persons who reenter the active service (including persons discharged to accept commissions), where such reentrance is a continuation of previous active service without interruption, must make application on Insurance Form 350a, which requires a complete report of physical examination. USE INK OR TYPE.

1. NAME IN FULL: (Please print or type) First: Courtney Middle: Dale Last name: Griffith

2. HOME ADDRESS: Number Street or rural route: RR 1 County, city, town, or post office: Lewis State: Ind

3. I WAS BORN AT City, town, or post office: Lewis State: Ind. Day of month: 18 Month: April Year: 1924 Age nearest birthday: 19

4. DATE OF ENTRY INTO PRESENT TOUR OF ACTIVE DUTY: [illegible] March 9th, 1943

5. PRESENT ORGANIZATION Rank, grade, or rating: Private Organization, regiment, station, ship, etc.: Unassigned

6. SERIAL NUMBER: 3509[illegible]179

7. DATE OF SEPARATION FROM LAST TOUR OF ACTIVE DUTY. (If no previous active duty, state "none.") none

8. ARE YOU NOW DISABLED ON ACCOUNT OF INJURY OR DISEASE? IF SO, STATE DETAILS

9. I HEREBY APPLY FOR INSURANCE ON THE FIVE-YEAR LEVEL PREMIUM TERM PLAN IN THE AMOUNT OF $ 10000

10. ARE YOU NOW CARRYING GOVERNMENT LIFE INSURANCE? (ANSWER "YES" or "NO") no IF "YES" GIVE AMOUNT OF INSURANCE AND POLICY NUMBER IF AVAILABLE. AMOUNT, $ ______ POLICY No. ______
(No person may carry a combined amount of National Service Life Insurance and U. S. Government Life Insurance in excess of $10,000 at any one time)

11. COMPLETE NAME OF EACH BENEFICIARY

11. Complete name of each beneficiary (If married woman, her own first and middle name and husband's last name must be stated)		Relationship	Amount of insurance to be paid to each beneficiary	Post-office address (Number and street, city, town, or post office and State)
PRINCIPAL	Courtney Lee Griffith	Father	10000	RR 1, Lewis, Ind.
CONTINGENT	Lillian Mae Griffith	Mother	10000	same as above

Permitted class of beneficiaries: Husband or wife, child, parent, brother, or sister of the insured. (For further information see reverse side, paragraph 2.)

12. I REQUEST THE POLICY BE MAILED TO—(Please print or type)
Courtney Lee Griffith (Full name) same as above (Address)

13. EFFECTIVE DATE OF INSURANCE (see reverse side, paragraph 1).
I REQUEST THAT THE EFFECTIVE DATE of this policy be made the 10th day of March 43, and

A. I enclose herewith remittance payable to the TREASURER OF THE UNITED STATES by ______ (Check, draft, or money order) in the amount of $ ______ in payment of the first ______ (Write above whether monthly, quarterly, semiannual, or annual) premium on the insurance, or

B. I will register an allotment of pay involving advance of active service pay under the provisions of Public Law 451, 77th Congress, in payment of the first monthly premium of $ 6.50 on the insurance, or

C. I will register an allotment of pay effective in the month in which application for insurance is signed, in payment of the first monthly premium of $ ______ on the insurance.

If an effective date is not specified by the applicant, the insurance herein applied for shall become effective as follows:
(a) If the first premium is paid by direct remittance or by advance of active service pay under the provisions of Public Law 451, 77th Congress, the insurance shall become effective as of the date on which valid application is signed and such premium is tendered.
(b) If the first premium is paid by regular allotment of pay effective in the month in which application for insurance is signed, the insurance shall become effective as of the first day of the month following the month in which valid application and such allotment are executed, provided the applicant is then in the active service and the amount of the premium is deducted from the applicant's service pay in accordance with the allotment.

THE UNITED STATES IS NOT LIABLE IF DEATH OCCURS PRIOR TO THE EFFECTIVE DATE OF THE POLICY

14. I WILL PAY SUBSEQUENT PREMIUMS IN THE MANNER AND AMOUNT INDICATED BELOW:

A. BY ALLOTMENT OF PAY MONTHLY	B. BY DIRECT REMITTANCE TO THE VETERANS ADMINISTRATION Monthly	Quarterly	Semiannually	Annually
$ 6.50	$	$	$	$

SIGNED AT H. Q. FT. BENJ. HARRISON, IND. ON THE 10th DAY OF March 1943

WITNESSED BY: and
INFORMATION AS TO SERVICE CERTIFIED BY:

______ (Applicant sign here. Do not print signature)

G.V.FALKENBERG 1ST LT INF. INSURANCE OFFICER
(Rank and organization. See reverse side, paragraph 4.)

NOTE.—Penalties for fraud in securing for self or another the issue or payment of insurance: $1,000 to $5,000 fine and imprisonment. Insurance will be forfeited for mutiny, treason, spying or other specified offenses. (Sections 613, 615, and 612, National Service Life Insurance Act of 1940.)

DO NOT USE THIS SPACE

Effective Date ______ Age ______ Amt. ______ Premium ______
Beneficiary ______
Action taken ______
Examiner ______ Reviewer ______
Certificate issued ______ Policy issued ______

16—30388-1

MONTHLY PREMIUMS FOR EACH $1,000 OF INSURANCE

FIVE-YEAR LEVEL PREMIUM TERM PLAN

Age	Monthly Premium	Age	Monthly Premium	Age	Monthly Premium	Age	Monthly Premium	Age	Monthly Premium
15	$0.63	25	$0.67	35	$0.76	45	$0.99	55	$1.77
16	.64	26	.68	36	.77	46	1.03	56	1.90
17	.64	27	.69	37	.79	47	1.08	57	2.05
18	.64	28	.69	38	.81	48	1.14	58	2.21
19	.65	29	.70	39	.83	49	1.20	59	2.40
20	.65	30	.71	40	.85	50	1.27	60	2.60
21	.65	31	.72	41	.87	51	1.35	61	2.82
22	.66	32	.73	42	.89	52	1.44	62	3.07
23	.66	33	.74	43	.92	53	1.54	63	3.34
24	.67	34	.75	44	.95	54	1.65	64	3.64

SPECIFIC INSTRUCTIONS.

1. The applicant should specify the exact date of the month on which he desires the insurance policy to become effective. Upon written request of the applicant the policy of insurance may be issued effective while the applicant is in the active service—(A) as of the date on which valid application is signed, provided there is tendered with the application a direct remittance in payment of the first premium or an allotment of pay, involving advance of active service pay under the provisions of Public Law 451, 77th Congress, in payment of the first monthly premium; (B) as of the first day of the month following the date valid application is signed and the first premium is tendered, if such premium is paid by a direct remittance or by an allotment of pay effective in the month in which application for insurance is signed; (C) as of the first day of the month in which valid application is signed and the first premium is tendered by a direct remittance; (D) as of the first day of any month, but not more than 6 months, prior to the month in which valid application is signed and the first premium is tendered by a direct remittance, provided that there be paid an amount equal to the full reserve on the insurance at the end of the month prior to the month in which the application for insurance is signed and the first premium for the month in which the application is signed.

2. The insurance may be applied for in favor of one or more of the following persons: Husband or wife, child (including adopted child, stepchild, or illegitimate child), parent (including parent through adoption and person who stood in loco parentis to the insured at any time prior to entry into active service for a period of not less than 1 year), brother or sister (including those of the half blood) of the insured.

The insured may name any person or persons within the permitted class as contingent beneficiary or beneficiaries who will take the monthly installments of insurance if the principal beneficiary or beneficiaries predecease the insured, or take any remaining monthly installments if the principal beneficiary or beneficiaries survive the insured but die before all installments certain have been paid.

3. The insurance shall be payable in the following manner:

(1) If the beneficiary to whom payment is first made is under 30 years of age at the time of maturity, in two hundred and forty equal monthly installments at the rate of $5.51 for each $1,000 of insurance.

(2) If the beneficiary to whom payment is first made is 30 or more years of age at the time of maturity, in equal monthly installments for one hundred and twenty months certain, with such payments continuing during the remaining lifetime of such beneficiary. The amount of the monthly installment for each $1,000 of insurance shall be determined by the age of the beneficiary at the date of the death of the insured.

(3) Any installments certain of insurance remaining unpaid at the death of any beneficiary shall be paid in equal monthly installments in an amount equal to the monthly installments paid to the first beneficiary, to the person or persons then in being within the classes hereinafter specified and in the order named, unless designated by the insured in a different order—

(A) to the widow or widower of the insured, if living;

(B) if no widow or widower, to the child or children of the insured, if living, in equal shares;

(C) if no widow, widower, or child, to the parent or parents of the insured who last bore that relationship, if living, in equal shares;

(D) if no widow, widower, child, or parent, to the brothers and sisters of the insured, if living, in equal shares.

If no beneficiary is designated by the insured or if the designated beneficiary does not survive the insured, the beneficiary shall be determined in accordance with the order specified in subparagraph (3) of the above, and the insurance shall be payable in equal monthly installments in accordance with subparagraphs (1) and (2) as the case may be.

4. This application must be witnessed and the information as to service certified by the commissioned officer who has custody of the applicant's service record unless by reason of detached service no commissioned officer is available, in which event it may be witnessed by a noncommissioned officer who, if he has custody of the applicant's service record, may certify the information as to service.

U. S. GOVERNMENT PRINTING OFFICE O 16—30380-1

Dear Dad & mom

Well I got my uniform today & it fits me
just fine. I have only about 10 min to
write this in so I will have to make it
short I sent my clothes away today. we
took our shots today got a clothes. that
is about all I may be on guard tomorrow
night 10:P.M until 11:A.M not bad, carry
a 45 & a 12-pup they ask me if I ever
shot a gun so you see I am fixed to work
while I am here. I called Norma last
night & I will call her again tonight. We
got up a 3:45 this morning isn't that early
I think so. We got our orders & what to
do & what not to do. You can't write because
I move all over this place. I look to
get taken out Fri or Sat. I may call
just before I leave if I can find time
this is my buddies pen he is a nice kid
to. We have been together all the time
since we been here. It is raining here now
& it is 8:P.M. I have to go down & see
if I can shoot. I will write when I
get time.

so long

Love
Dale.

Dear, Dad & Mother. March 15, 1943

How is everyone just fine I hope, Well I have been on this train since Sat at 7:15 I am in the bad land's of Dakota now I think we are going to Wash. We left & we went to St. Louis. We went from there to a threw Mo. then over to Ken. up to Iowa then Nebr. then we are where we are now about 75 miles south of N. D. we will be there in an hour. We followed the Mo. river a long ways, Dad you should of seen the Duck's geese, grouse, Prairie chicken's Phesants all kind of them if I had of had my shot gun talk about shooting all them I mention you sure could get action. We are not allowed off of the train eat sleep & everything on it. In Nebr. we went along some river, & you never seen the water for duck's & geese, that wouldn't even fly we got to see their eye's 50 feet to some of them where the train was close to the river. The Prairie Chicken are really thick in Nebr. One place I remember the most, an old rail fence

& it was covered with them within a 100 feet of them. Talk about going threw the bad land's, This is rough county go threw pass'es & tunnels Pheasant's are mostly in nebr, some up here one other kind of a bird I never have found out the name of it yet. In places you can see for miles & miles. When I get back Dad you an I are going to nebr, a fishing & hunting I don't know them hills in owen county about half way get you down, then you haven't any business out here. There is a little snow up here in places but it isn't so cold. we rode yesterday with the windows down. Well good bye I am going to see more of the bad land's.

Love
Dale

627 T.H. Q.M. C. Refig Fixes (SERIAL no 35096179)
Butcher Platoon
this was on envelope

Dear Dad & Mother

Well all is fine. ever way you look there is Mts. I can't tell you what I am doing it is not allowed out. I can tell you that after my 4 weeks of training I will go to school. Our train went into Wash. I le[ft] off a group of men. I sure have seen some pretty country out here, but it isn't like home. I am with 3 or there is three of us from Brazil all together we sleep side by side. Dad I seen some wild deer in the Mts. there must of been 30 of them all in one bunch. I sure would of liked to been there with a gun. Us three boys are going to have our pictures taken & sent to the Brazil Times. I like it better here than I did at Fort Ben. There is about 60,000 in this camp but we or there is 74 of us in a divison by itself you have to be a perfect man to get into this group so out of 60,000 I was one of the 74 so you see I am or supposed to be a good man. I will try to write every day about something I don't know what about. We were on the train from Sat. night until Thursday at 2:00 in the evening. Well good bye I am going to write to Norma.

Love
Dale

We're depending on you!

A man you love is serving in our Armed Forces. For his protection, and for the protection of our whole war effort, we ask you to read carefully the message on the other side of this leaflet. Today our fighting men have the best training and equipment. They need one thing more . . . protection against careless talk.

Chief of Staff, United States Army.

16—32375-1

Don't let careless talk get there first ! ! !

Now that we're attacking, we must be doubly sure that careless talk doesn't give away our battle plans.

Don't talk about where soldiers or sailors are located, where they're going or when, what training they are being given or what equipment they use. Such facts help the enemy foresee our plans and prepare against them.

Remember that anything you may know about our Armed Forces or war production is confidential . . . unless it has been printed or broadcast on the radio.

Remember that Axis agents piece together *little* scraps of conversation to learn *big* military secrets.

If that happens our battle casualties will be greater . . . the war will last longer. Don't risk the life of your serviceman. Be careful what you say. Think before you talk.

WAR DEPARTMENT, WASHINGTON, D. C.

U. S. GOVERNMENT PRINTING OFFICE 16—32375-1

KNOWN IN CAMP AS THREE HOOSIERS

Left to right: Pvt. Harold "Shorty" Underwood, Pvt. Dale Griffith, Pvt. Stanley Eldridge.

These Brazilians are known in their camps as "The Three Hoosiers." They are proud to be in uniform and anxious to get into the fightin' to help bring this war to a

Camp White Oregon
(Post, camp, or station)

March 19, 1943
(Date)

NOTICE OF CHANGE OF ADDRESS

This is to advise you that my correct address now is:

Private Courtney D. Griffith 35196179
(Grade) (Name) (Army Serial No.)

627 Q.M. Refrig Fipd
(Organization) (Name of P. O. or A. P. O. number)

Signature Courtney D. Griffith

This is for the convenience of the soldier in advising his correspondents of his assignment to a unit or installation. A maximum of three of these cards will be issued to each soldier by his unit commander if he desires, within 15 days of his arrival at his new permanent station.

W. D., A. G. O. Form No. 204
October 1, 1941

16—24611-1 U. S. GOVERNMENT PRINTING OFFICE

WAR DEPARTMENT
THE ADJUTANT GENERAL'S OFFICE
WASHINGTON, D.C.
OFFICIAL BUSINESS

MAR 20 10 30 AM 1943

PENALTY FOR PRIVATE USE TO AVOID PAYMENT OF POSTAGE, $300

Mr. Courtney Griffith
Lewis
Indiana

Sun. March 21, 1943

Dear, Dad & Mother,

Well how is everything going home alright I hope, I sure wish I were there now these Sun. sure are long out here. It really is hot in the day time & very cold at night. Has or are you plowing yet dad I could stand a little of that now don't think I couldn't. Mother will you please send me some of those clothes hangers I really need them bad. This camp is in a valley I guess you would call it but there is mts. all around, There is snow on 2 high peaks out here. No tree's no nothing all you see is buildings & mts not much too look at. I guess we won't be here more than 3 mo. be shipped to some other camp. How is old pud alright I hope tell him if I were there I would lick him. Talk about your fishing dad I sure seen plenty of good river's & ponds to fish in out here. Then deer I told you about there were 7 buck's I seen & probably there were [illegible] I didn't see [illegible] was a real train ride. We play ball & about everything out here in the evening. You know you are 2 hrs. ahead of
us

2

us out here. The war sure sounds good doesn't it eve Serg. & even the captain told us we didn't have anything to worry about they all think it will be over by fall. I hope so anyway. Dad I am not flying airplanes or in the infantry or riding horses if I would go across the pond I would be a way back I know that now I am in a fixed division and a new group starting all together so if I get a rating I will really have a good chance to get to train other new men. We just get four weeks of training & then we go to school for about 6 weeks. There is about 6 opening & there is 74 of us I hope I am one of the lucky 6 I sure am going to try & try hard. We get paid out here on the tenth day of each. Dad I can send you $35 a month for I really don't need it. Don't get out of here. & so I couldn't spend it. I really don't have time to write to everyone for I don't have time but I will try. Well I must close. Love Dale.

March 22, 43

CAMP WHITE
OREGON

Dear Mother & Dad,

I got your letter today & was so glad to get. I am getting along alright as far as I know. Yes mother I have good eats & plenty. even have pies but they are not like your's mother. I got a letter from Targetti also today. My uniform fits me fine I wish you could see me I will have a picture taken & sent to you. Mother please don't send any more money for I really don't need it. I & two other boy's were in the same rooms, me & the other boy came in & Joe was his name was hanging from a rafter by his tie hung himself & also cut his throat with a razor, I can still see it. I & Fred took him down the Sgt helped us carry him out. There has been 6 others run off. Our job is too

find them. This is a new camp first
one's too live in this building, I never
have got over seeing all of them dear
I guess boy dad & sure would like
to had a gun well I have seen a lot
of things I never seen before & probably
will see a lot more. Don't forget to
send me my steel clothes hangers
Has dad plowed any yet or is it too
wet. I thought it rain out here
all the time it hasn't rained since
I been here. Well good bye &
write I'll try to write as often as
I can. Tell fred to be a good boy

Love Dale.

Mon. night

P.S. I am going to be,

I also got your letter sent to fort Ben.

Sun. March 28, 43

CAMP WHITE
OREGON

Dear Dad & Mother.

How are getting now dad I sure hope a lot better for it isn't going to be long before you start plowing I wish I was there doing it for me & you always did get along fine sometimes I wanted to go to town or I shot up a lot of shells or beat you killing quails or left a ear of corn but sum it all up we made out fine. I had my picture taken today but it will be 3 or 4 weeks before you get them one big one I sure hope it is a good one. Did you or have you been getting all of my letters or not I sure hope so I try to write ever day if I can at all or if I find time. I am going to try I write to Pete this evening if I can get time I don't get to go hunting the mans mother is very sick. Mother I have a real nice buddy Robert Miller from Indianapolis he doesn't drink smoke or nothing. He is married has been for 3 yrs. He really is a good boy. This place as I told you is surrounded with Mts. all covered with snow & ever green trees it sure is pretty but not like being in the river bottom & looking around. We have very nice officers here & really good eats. I never have got the hangers yet but I should get them soon or I hope so I never got a letter from no one Fri or Sat. Has Mama been down lately I expect all of her's was air mail so I expect she sent the other's just by mail so I'll be getting them Mon. or Tues. I walked down to a Mt stream yesterday evening & wish you were there with your fishing outfit dad I bet you could do real good. Well I must stop. Love

Dale

P.S. How is Bud have him to write

April, 1, 43.

Dear Dad & Mother.

I am O.K. got a card from Harold & Norma & Clint. I had another tooth filled today & she sure is hurting. I bad about old Jack dying. Was dad or are you plowing yet dad. It sure is hot out here in these parts. We went over the Mts. today I think several of them fell out but I was right there till the finish. The war is going good out here, it looks in our favor & lets hope it stays that way. you know I really would like to go across the pond just to see what all is over there, I won't go until I have to & I don't think I'll have too. Miller my buddy is shining his shoes now, he sure is a nice kid. I have too write to Norma Harold & Clint yet tonight or I should I'll find me

time to write to Norma I'll bet you
I haven't resaived you hangers yet I
will soon I hope I have been getting
all of your letter's do you get mine
I hope so, Dad I seen lot's of deer
today I had a gun but no shells I
would of liked to crack down on
one, I bet I do some day. I may get
to this Sun. I hope. For supper I had
fruit Salad (S.P.) mashed potato, roll's beans
& ice cream not bad. Here is that
Ky. if he isn't a real one can't do
nothing except play poker. Well
good bye. Love Dale

P.S. Tell Fred to write me a letter

April fool!

May 3, 43

U. S. ARMY

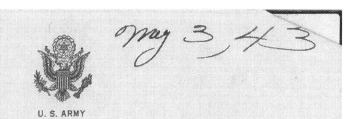

Dear Dad & Mother,

Well how is everyone I am fine I haven't done much today, went to school all day I guess I will go to school here for 13 weeks a long time I sure wish I was out of this place in a way but I would hate to leave, my new girl but they are all alike none of them worth a ___. after my 13 weeks I may get to come home for 14 days I sure hope so. Dad & Bugs will have to take me a fishing. I got your letters today one from Tangel & Clint, Clint has to tell me how to live you know his line. How is the bass fishing pretty good, I'll tell you Sun Shine they are biting out here Boy! Dad I sure wish you & Bugs were here to fish a couple of weeks you sure could catch some I know. Well good night

Love
Dale

May 6, 43

U. S. ARMY

Dearest Dad & Mother & Bud,

Well how is everyone I am fine
I sent you a big picture, I hope
you like it write & tell me if you
do or not. I gave Ruby one, she said
she was going to send it to Hollywood
her & I went to a big dance you
should of seen me hot stuff. I
wrote to Jackie & Bugs to-night too.
I went to school this morning &
this evening I went to Portland, to
a machine shop, I guess that is what
I'll do for awhile. I also got my G. I.
drivers licens to-day, I can drive truck
cars or anything now. Have you got my
plugs yet dad or not, I expect you have.
or at least you should of. Well ~~mother~~ dear

2

& Dad I can't think of nothing else
to write so I will close but I'll try
to write ever day. Lots of Love

Dale

May 10, 43

U. S. ARMY

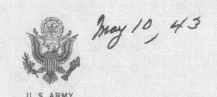

Dear Dad & Mother,
Well here it is Mon. night hows is ever
one I am fine, Well they changed me
today & put me inspection meat at a
slaughter house in Grant Pass it is
about 32 miles from here I don't know
how they ever picked me & a Ross
kid he is a Serg. so we have a big
time all we do is go up & sat down
all day a nice job. I guess this 2. M.
they put you any place. Any way I will
have a good Job, The reason I got moved
the army started buying meat threw this
packing house & it called for a inspector
out of our outfit so the Cap. called me in
& said for me too take over today so I
went I sure have it easy. I wear a
white coat & pants & a little tie I look
like a dude, I'll have my picture made
in them & send them all we done today
was walk from the killing room
over

to where they boned the meat & there is
a couple of nice looking girls work in
the office so I am not so bad of or the
Serg. says we are lucky, I also will
get my stripe's I know for sure so keep
still until I do, I work in side & the
Serg in the pen's where the live hogs
& cattle come in the shoot. Here too get
up a little early but I don't mind.
How is Dad, I bet he is a dandy. Oh
yes I got the sweetest letter from my
Darling little Bonnie today. Tony this
& that I say A. S. the G [illegible] her
If they do you or me that way once well
Ill with them, I don't mind getting shit
on but I won't let any women rub it
in. If she ever gets on her knees well I
will still kick her in the face. Well
this all the paper I have L. I must get
to bed as I will be up at 4:30.

Lots
of
Love
Dale,

May 14, 1943

UNITED STATES ARMY

Dearest Mother & Dad,

Well how is everyone, I hope fine. Well the old war looks good doesn't it I hope she hurries up & ends. so I can come home. I got two letter's from Irene today, I don't know why she write for I never went with her only 3 times. How is Fred a big boy now I bet, is Jack & Bud keeping it down there I bet they are, How is Jerry growing to be a big boy. Say! have you ever got my big picture yet I expect you should of by now. Mother you said a girl lady won wasn't any good well don't worry for I know the ropes on girl's don good now so don't worry. This letter may seem short & funny but it is time for

2

UNITED STATES ARMY

bed & I don't have any news. Only I am still working at a packing house. I'll write in the morning if I can find time. So good-bye. A lot of love

[illegible]

May 20 - 43

Dear Dad & Mother,

How is everyone I am fine I just came in & thought I had better write I also want to show you a picture of a fighter me & Ruby are going to Fri night, I didn't know she liked to go to fights & besides she bought us a ring side seat can you imagine that they were only $32 a seat so I'll really be up in the money won't I. Dad I wish you were going for you really could see a real fight once. I sure have seen lot of things that I wouldn't of never seen if I wasn't here now but I would rather be driving the old tractor. I sure do hate it about raining there all the time did they get any fish if I were there I would get a mess. I'll never forget the time I killed all the ducks in the old pond.

over

2

I hope I get to go to Owen County this
fall & bet you killing the grays. you
know I can do it & also get the
biggest bass. I am going to get me a shot
gun & kill some of the Pheasant out
here there sure are a lot of them. Well
I must stop for I am going over to the
river & drag me out a fish a 10 lber
The only trouble I have to turn him loose
for I have no place to fry him tonight
I wish you were here Dad, I could show
you more game & big game in 15 min. than
you ever seen all your life ha, Well I'll
tell you my luck,

Love

Dale

June 3-43

Dearest Dad & Mother,

How is everyone I am just fine. Fri
we go out under machine gun fire
It fires 36 in. over your head. We
have to crawl for a 100 yards on our
stomach & a 90 lb. pack on our back
I guess it is plenty stuff but I believe
I could do anything now. How is Jud
is he still growing, I bet I won't know
him when I get home. I haven't heard
from Jack & Bugs for a month, what
is the matter our they mad or something? I have been so busy the last
three days I haven't had time to
write I have been up at 4 ever.
morning & I don't get back here until
9 at night so you see I haven't had

over

any time at all. I guess it will go a
little easier now. We had a large shipment
to make so we had to stay on the job.

You should get a bond real soon
if I don't get it by the 15th be sure
& let me know & if you need it cash
it in for it is all right. Have we got
any corn planted yet? I hope so. I'll
be alright when I get out of the army
I'll get a license as a gov. meat inspector
& that pays 60 a week buy me a new
shotgun 410 ga. that is where my second
1/10 goes for I expect Dad you would rather
have your hundred that way also. I
got you card today if they ain't dead
they soon will be, I hope! Well I
must close with lots of love & luck

Dale

P.S. The fish ain't biting so hot.

June 17-43

UNITED STATES ARMY

Dearest Dad & Mother, & Bud.

How is everyone I am just fine the only thing I think I am about getting tired of this army. I worked this morning & sleep this evening they never had anything to do at the slaughter house so me & Serg. sleep. The fellow that runs the place took our picture yesterday I hope it is good. I think he got part of the cattle in it. I got your letter today, I wish I could of seen Jr. I will get a furlough soon, They start the 26 of this month, we draw numbers & the little no. goes first. It takes or would take $85 for me to get there we get five days at home. Say have you ever got that bond yet you should of by now if you are going too. Boy it sure is

we

hot here now 120 plenty warm, we had a
black out last night from 1 to 3 this morning
couldn't talk smoke or hardly move, I don't
think much of it. I have almost back
out on that Cadet outfit for that is a
sure way to go across, I think we will
get moved from here right away so maybe
I could be closer home, Have we got all of
the corn planted yet I sure hope so, How is
my & Bud's colt I bet she is a big horse now.

Have fixed to write Iwan to see if he
still can write or not Tell Jack & Bugs Hello
I must stop for I want to take a shower.

Love
Ref

June 14, 43,

Medford Slaughter house.

P.F.C. Courtney Griffith

P.F.C. Clarence Creasy,

Medford Oregon,

A poor place to be &

I know

938L

June 27, 43

UNITED STATES ARMY

Dearest Dad & Mother & Bud,

How is everyone I am just fine say! Dad I bet I got it on you I caught a 7 lb salmon, that will hold you won't it I was going to have mine Ruby's picture taken with it but we couldn't find any films I was standing out on a rock when I hooked him Ruby & her dad where up the river a little ways I yelled look here what I got he started out where I was & fell in & lost his rod & reel & did he ever carry-on HaHa we are going to have him for supper. I wish you were here, some day we are

over

coming out here shoot deer & catch fish
& look for more dears no not that
but we could have a fine time. Well
it is for sure I will be home in
a month at the most & maybe sooner
that is if I get the money. I talked
to the captain this morning & he said
there was a Sgt rating coming out
real soon just keep on the ball &
keep that dum no good girl off of your
mind & I think everything will come your
way so that sounds alright & how.
How is the corn I bet I wont know
things around there. Well I must
close

Love

Dale

August 5, 43

Dear Dad & Mother,

How is everyone I am just fine. I was up this morning at 4 & walked to the Pistol range but it started raining & I never got to shoot today. Has it ever rained there yet or is it still dry & hot. I sure was glad to see the rain here for it is the first since April. Have you cut any hay yet or has the fish started to hit? or the red tail to thigh? That is your part dad or is Fred doing the fishing now. I should be able to catch one Fri E. for I haven't even gotten a bump last night or this morning. I can't find a cane pole to put the rod in so I guess I'll have to put it between two stick some way. I seen the old man at Medford to-night & he is going to get me some

deer horns. Dad you will have
to take some sand paper & shellack
& fix them up & put them over
the double door. I did know
they might already be fixed up
he never said. I lost my plug
last night dad I'll see if I can find
another hopper. Well I known as
usual this long hod but I can think
of anything to write.

Love

Dale

Sept. 1, 43

Dearest Dad & Mother

How is everyone I am fine, we took a train load of stuff out, is the reason I haven't written sooner. I am sending the $10 for Pud too buy his boot's with & will try & send him ten every month from now on while he is in school & Chad will buy his pencils &c &c. I am going to the show to-night I am going with a bunch of boys for we all have too get up early tomorrow morning & we will have to go back for bed early. I have had a little cold not bad I got it I think from my ride. I sure had a nice time & seen lot of

Calif. Well the boys are ready so I must close I'll write tomorrow.

Love
Dale

Sept. 8, 43.

UNITED STATES ARMY

Dearest Dad & Mother,

How is everyone over the trip to Owen County. Did Paul kill as many as I would of? I never got any letter from you today. I think the mail gets all messed up some way. That sure was good news about Italy wasn't it. One down & two to go. Ha Ha. I am working on a ice box at Ashland now putting in 7 motors ect. pipes & a water system. When we get that fixed I reckon I.

over

3

will go back to Grand Pass & work. Well, I have found another girl now Mickie is her name. Ruby went to Calif to college. I got two letters a day from her but I wrote & told her I was my mommy's boy Ha Ha. Mickie doesn't have a car but her pa does & give me another week & I will be driving it Ha Ha. I found my pocket book I had put it in my own coat pocket. I keep stamps ect. in it & when I was looking for a stamp to put on the card I sent I found it. Have you got the bond for this month yet or not. If

U. S. ARMY

Jun, 8, 43

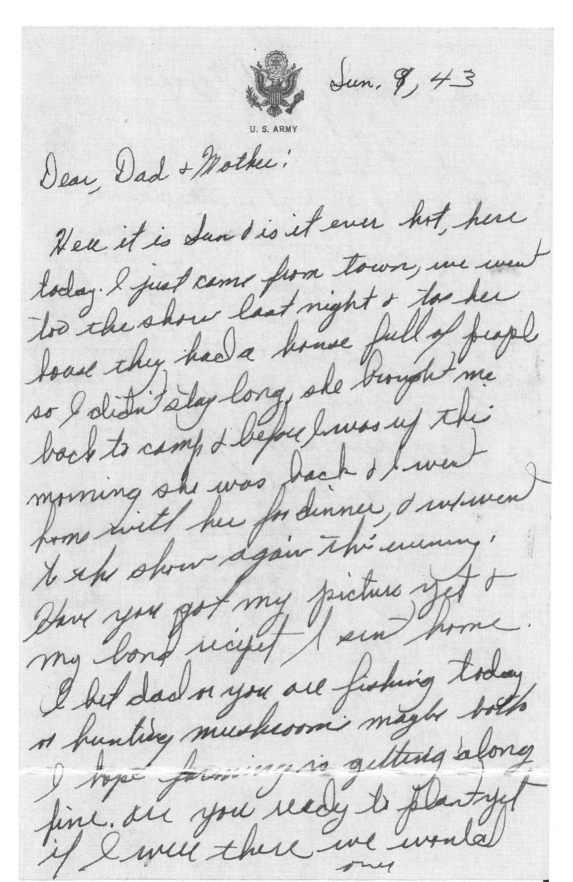

Dear, Dad & Mother;

Well it is Sun & is it ever hot, here today. I just came from town, we went to the show last night & too her house they had a house full of people so I didn't stay long, she brought me back to camp & before I was up the morning she was back & I went home with her for dinner, & we went to the show again this evening.
Have you got my picture yet & my bond receipt I sent home.
I bet dad & you are fishing today or hunting mushrooms maybe both. I hope farming is getting along fine. are you ready to plant yet if I were there we would

over

2

be ready to plant. Well I guess for
sure I will get to come home in
12 week's it will cost $65 for a
round ticket but it will be worth
it I will have to save my money.
I have a real good chance to get
my stripes I think they will be
passed out in 3 or 4 week's a Cpl
gets $66 a month I sure hope I make
it. Well I have a lot of letters to
write so I must close

Love
Dale

P.S. How is old Bud I bet he
is a little man now.

Sept. 21, 43

Dearest Dad & Mother,

I got two letters from you today & one from Margaret. I am still working in town. The first of October I am going too send you a $100 to pay for my furlough. I have been doing pretty good. We work 40 hrs. that goes to the Co. & we don't get paid for it & all over that we get at 80¢ hr. We work in town it is a big ice & cold storag plant. They have a lot of pears they cool & ship out on box cars & we get paid all over 40 hrs. a week. It will stop around the 10th of Oct. so I should make a couple hundred so I can send you $50 & have enough for my next furlough

if I get one & I hope I do around
Christmas. I hope you got the other
$10 I sent. I am sending Pud a buck
he can buy him a new shirt. Well
I had better close for it is getting
late so when you get the $100 pay my
furlough off. I'll send it by a wire
I'll try & write tomorrow night

Lots of Love

Dale

Oct. 10, 43

CAMP WHITE
OREGON

Dearest Dad & Mother,

How is everyone I am just fine. I went to town last night. I bought me a new pocket book & signed up for the book for you Dad. You won't get it until Dec. as the Nov. is already sent out. Got me some socks, toilet brush holder ect. I hope you got the money order O.K. I am putting $50 away so if I get another furlough I'll have the money if you need it let me know. I told you they were breaking our Co. up they did & now there is only 135 of us our

I don't know what that means
but I have an idea. How is
Pud? Has he got a spanking
yet. or got put out 3 days to
go duck hunting. HAHA.
How is Jack & Bugs? I will
get a chance to write them
now since I am not working
in town. We are going on a
problem next week I expect
we will go out about 100 miles
or so. I had better close
for I have to shower & go get a
hair-cut. I'll write tomorrow

Lot of
Love
Dale

Dearest Folks:

How is everyone O.K. I hope
as I am. I got a letter from
you today & one yesterday. Rem. the
Mishler girl I used to go with
I got a letter from her too.
I wish you were here tomorrow
night Dad & see Joe L. I sure
am going I'll send you the
picture Ho Ho. I guess the
winter "rains" has started
for it is raining here like it
does there in April. I am
going to the show tonight
[illegible]
with Bob. Well I
had better close as it is
almost time to go. You will

be getting that fishing rod next
week sometime. I got the
paper today. Love
Dad

CAMP WHITE
OREGON

Dear Folks,

Well we found out we will get furlough again but don't know for sure when but by Xmas maybe we hope. I may get more days I hope. I haven't much time to write as Millie & I are going to the show. How is Dad? Tell him if I get too come to have are gun oiled up [illegible]. That rifle is on it way. Well I have to stop write tomorrow

Love
Lee

CAMP WHITE
OREGON
MEDFORD, OREG.
NOV 2
3-PM
1943
Mr & Mrs Courtney Griffith
Lewis
Indiana

CAMP WHITE
OREGON

Jun. 23

Dear Folks,

It is really raining here today but it is really warm & the grass is green as ever.

I am sending these papers be sure & keep them. That Ten is for candy HaHa. I have these $5. bonds so you can cash them or don't be afraid to do so if you need them, for I want you too. We don't know for sure yet when we are going but I expect it will be in the next week or so. We will go to some City where the stuff is sent &

see that it is O.K. before it goes
to the front. so you don't have
to worry because we will
be away back there. We got
all our new clothes' ect. next
week. My arm is a little
sore, I have had enough needles
stuck in me to last awhile.
Three in one day & four more
to take. I'll send the suitcase
home tomorrow I think I'll get
the rest this week to. We sure
had a nice dinner today that
is one thing we always have
plenty to eat. Hank & I went
to the show last night. They
took our three day pass away
from us, no one can leave

CAMP WHITE
OREGON

camp now, you know I told you I would get some pictures. I have been trying ever since I came back, but I can't get them. Here they are 6 mos. ahead all the time. How is Pue. & school right I hope. I sure like it if you never did get the pict. I sent maybe you will if you haven't already for it has never came back here. But of the boys send none of the boys the boys send none got there. I don't believe 1/2 of them ever get out of camp. They built a big bowling alley here, so us boys spend

lot of time there. It is just
10¢ a game. I think Hank
wants to go up to-night so
I expect that is where we will
go. Well I must close but
I'll write tomorrow you be
sure & write Love

Dale

Dearest Folk's

How is everyone fine I hope
I am O.K. I got your letter
today the first in five days'

I am glad you are getting the
new stove, maybe Bud won't
freeze this winter. I really
don't know about the furlough
as I wrote before if we don't
get moved I will get another
one around Christmas or I hope
I will. I don't know what I'll
do tomorrow go to town or sleep
as I get the day off. Sat. is
"Pay day" I'll get about 30. about one
trip to Calif. Ha Ha. I did meet
a real good looking girl down

there. Have to do something for
you can't sat here & think about
the old girl friends or you would
be nuts HxHx. The longer you
stay away it gives you a chance
to forget them. This Pay day
I'll sign you up with Hunters
land. I know you can't sit by
that new stove & read it HxHx
Well I must close as it is
late I'll write tomorrow night

Love
Dad

MEDFORD, OREG.
NOV 15
10 30 AM
1943
AIR MAIL
Mr. & Mrs. Courtney Griffith
Lewis
Indiana

Dec. 9,

Dear Folks,

I haven't heard from you the last two days but maybe the mail never came thru; I looked all over town yesterday for something I could send you for Xmas but I can't find a thing that I could send, I bought Mickie a little pen for 3$ bucks that is the most I am ever going to spend on any girl. I guess I will be working here for 2 wks checking meat into the ware house. It rained a little today the first day it hasn't rained all day for a month. Are you done with the

corn yet, or the shells. Have
you got the book yet I send for
if not tell me & I will go down
& get on the old man. It looks
like we are going to be here
yet next summer for the Cap
was telling us what all we
had to do the next 6 mos. I
guess he has got Hank Miller
& I lined up for Wash starting
March to May, so I guess I'll
be here yet when the war is
over. Well I must close as it
is pretty late I'll write tomorrow

Lots of
Love
Dale

CAMP WHITE
OREGON

Dear Folks,
How is everyone just fine I hope
I am O.K. & doing well, I think
I got a letter from everyone
I know except you today. Mama
Margaret Irene B. Mickie Agnes S.
Evelyn Gareen & Ruth, so you see
I am pretty well know & they all
tell me this is leap year ha ha.
but who cares. Has Bud got his
letter yet? We never done much
today we got our new clothes
in est. We don't know for sure
when we will leave but real
soon. I heard over the radio
where we get $300 when we

get out of the army, with that
& the bonds I can get a tractor.
or a wife one. I belive I will
take the tractor ####. It sure
has been a pretty day here nice
& warm. We played ball this
morning. I am keeping my watch
ect. so I guess we won't be
where it is so tuff. Well I must
close for I am going to the
show. Lots of love
Dale

Fri. 21

Dear Folks,

I thought is was about time I
was writting. We haven't had time
to do anything the last week. This
is the first letter I have written
in five days. I got two letters from
you today took a week to get them
by air mail. I am going to send this
one free I think you will get them
just as quick. I wish I were there
to eat some of that fresh ham. We
get ham about twice a week here.
We had steak green beans potatoes ec
for supper to-night. I sure am going
to town 187 lbs now & 5'10½" bare
footed. I will make six feet in another
year. How is Bud tell him I got
his letter. I bet he is really getting

4

big. We got a new jeep so we are
fixed up until we move. I went
over to the P.X an got a hair cut
so when I got this wrote I am
going to take a shower & go to bed.
Hank an I got three days off starting
Mon. we have got 6 so I guess we
will stay right here. We have our
orders to turn in a lot of stuff so
I really think we will move in the
next month so don't worry if you don't
hear from me. They say here that the
second front has started in Europe. I hope
it is true, but the radio hasn't said anything
so we will wait & see. Well I must
close I'll write tomorrow. Hope everyone
is O.K. mother

Lot of Love
Dale

Jan. 28

Dear Folks,

I got a letter today
I was very glad to
get it for it has been
a week.

Have you got the fishing
rod yet? I think he
finally send it. I am
sending a bunch of
other stuff Mon. We
sure have been on the
run. We have to pack
all of our stuff in the
duffle bag & fall out &
take everything out & pack

2

it back in, I guess
he wants us to know
how to put things in
it. He told us today we
wouldn't be here in
two weeks so I guess
we go. We got all new
clothes yesterday I sure
got a good fit.
What do you think of
this case. The Cap said
if you want them to
know where you are
going send this to

3

pop. I sure got a
good rifle I can hit a
bull's eye at 450 yds.
It sure has a kick to
it. I must close as it
is late I'll write tomorrow

Love

Dad

be real soon.
We had some pictures taken today, our Co. & the Vet. Co. I will send them to you when we get them. Well they put us off another two wks. maybe we will end up staying here after all but I don't expect we will.
I bought a new pen or did I tell you that last night. I mailed the

suitcase & the fishing rod
handle today. Have you
ever gotten the rock
yet or not.?
I will get a $14 raise
when we leave here.
so I will make it just
fine. We had steak for
supper to-night so I
am getting plenty to
eat. Well I must close
for this time. Hank & I
are going to the show.
Love Dale

Feb 2,

Dear Folks,

I don't know what I am going to write about this time but just to say hello

I hope ever one is well.

I am just fine.

I wrote Jackie a letter tonight I got a letter from you & her today.

I sure wish I were there to eat some of Terry's pie, maybe I will

Pfc. Dale Griffith
MEDFORD, OREG.
FEB 3
10:30AM
1944
Mr. & Mrs. Courtney Griffith
Lewis
Indiana
VIA
AIR MAIL

Sun. 6

Dear Folks;

I am sending you a little picture it isnt so good but just the same it is me.

It sure is a pretty here today the sun is shinning real bright & the birds are singing, just like spring there.

I havent found any Valentine's no where I know old Bud will be looking for one. I will keep on trying to find some.

2

How is the fox hunting coming along now? I sure wish I were there to kill one. I rem. last winter I tracked one for five miles around & when I came back there wasn't anyone there to kill him.

I got a letter to write Billy S. today for I got one from him this week so I expect I better ans. it today. I have to write Uncle Pete also. I am going to the show tonight.

3

I will pay you that $20 back when I get paid all I hope is that I get it before we leave.

Did you find the hayrode or not?

I think I will get me a tractor when I get out or a new car one.

I really want to go to police school too so I expect that is what I'll do as long as Bugs helps you. Well I will close but I'll write tomorrow.

Love
Dale

Sun. Feb 27-44

Dear Folks,

I don't know how long this letter will turn out to be, but just the same I will try to get at least one page.

I am just fine & hope you are all the same. I have been getting your letters just fine, But if you write V-mail I shall get them a lot sooner & will be more likely to get them.

How is Pud & school? Tell him to be a good boy & don't try to go duck hunting when he is to be in school ha ha. Why don't you get him the Pony? Tell him he can trade his colt for it if he wants to. If you see Chuck tell him I rec. his letter yesterday & I will write to him as soon as I can or when I find time. I wish I could tell you what is going on but I can't so I will have to forget about that.

I bought me a pipe this morning & I almost got sick, I guess it is too much for me.

I wrote Norma a letter yet I thought maybe I had better & I have to write Irene D. I have gotten a bunch of letters from her. I got your letter telling about you getting the fur & gloves. Well I must close & don't worry for I am just fine & will make it O.K.

Love

Dale

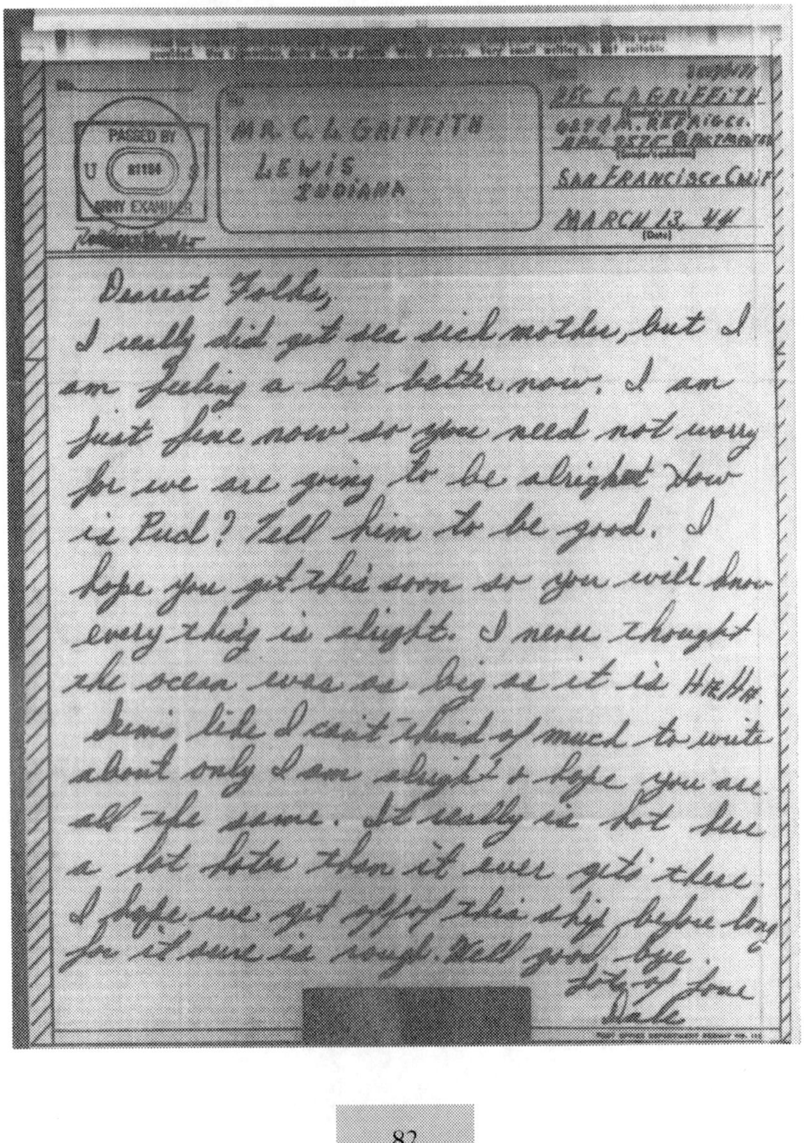
PASSED BY
U S
ARMY EXAMINER

MR. C. L. GRIFFITH
LEWIS
INDIANA

PFC C. A. GRIFFITH
SAN FRANCISCO CALIF
MARCH 13, 44
(Date)

Dearest Folks,
I really did get sea sick mother, but I am feeling a lot better now. I am just fine now so you need not worry for we are going to be alright. How is Bud? Tell him to be good. I hope you get this soon so you will know every thing is alright. I never thought the ocean was as big as it is HaHa. Seems like I can't think of much to write about only I am alright & hope you are all the same. It really is hot here a lot hotter than it ever gets there. I hope we get off of this ship before long for it sure is rough. Well good-bye.
Lots of Love
Dale

[redacted]

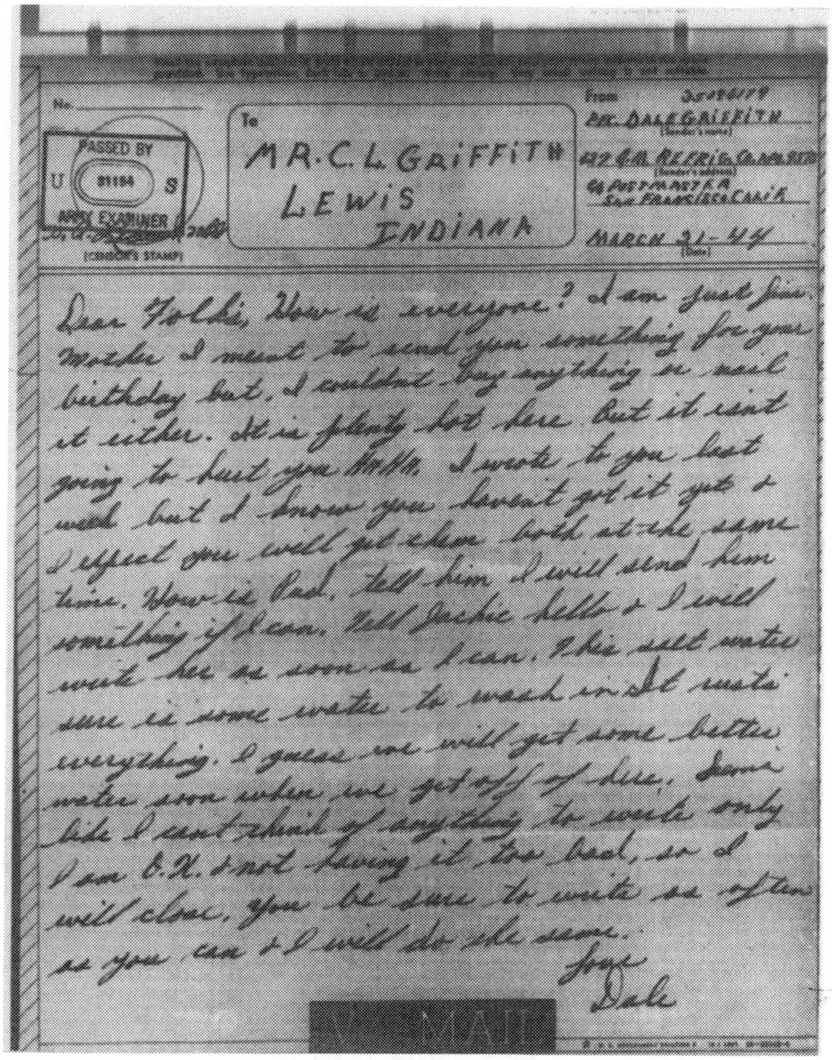
To
MR. C. L. GRIFFITH
LEWIS
INDIANA

From 35…
Pvt. DALE GRIFFITH
…
c/o POSTMASTER
San Francisco Calif.
MARCH 21-44

PASSED BY
U 81184 S
ARMY EXAMINER
(CENSOR'S STAMP)

Dear Folks, How is everyone? I am just fine.
Mother I meant to send you something for your
birthday but, I couldnt buy anything or mail
it either. It is plenty hot here but it isnt
going to hurt you HaHa. I wrote to you last
week but I know you havent got it yet &
I expect you will get them both at the same
time. How is Dad. Tell him I will send him
something if I can. Tell Jackie hello & I will
write her as soon as I can. This salt water
sure is some water to wash in It wate
everything. I guess we will get some better
water soon when we get off of here. Seems
like I cant think of anything to write only
I am O.K. & not having it too bad, so I
will close, you be sure to write as often
as you can & I will do the same.
Love
Dale

V-MAIL

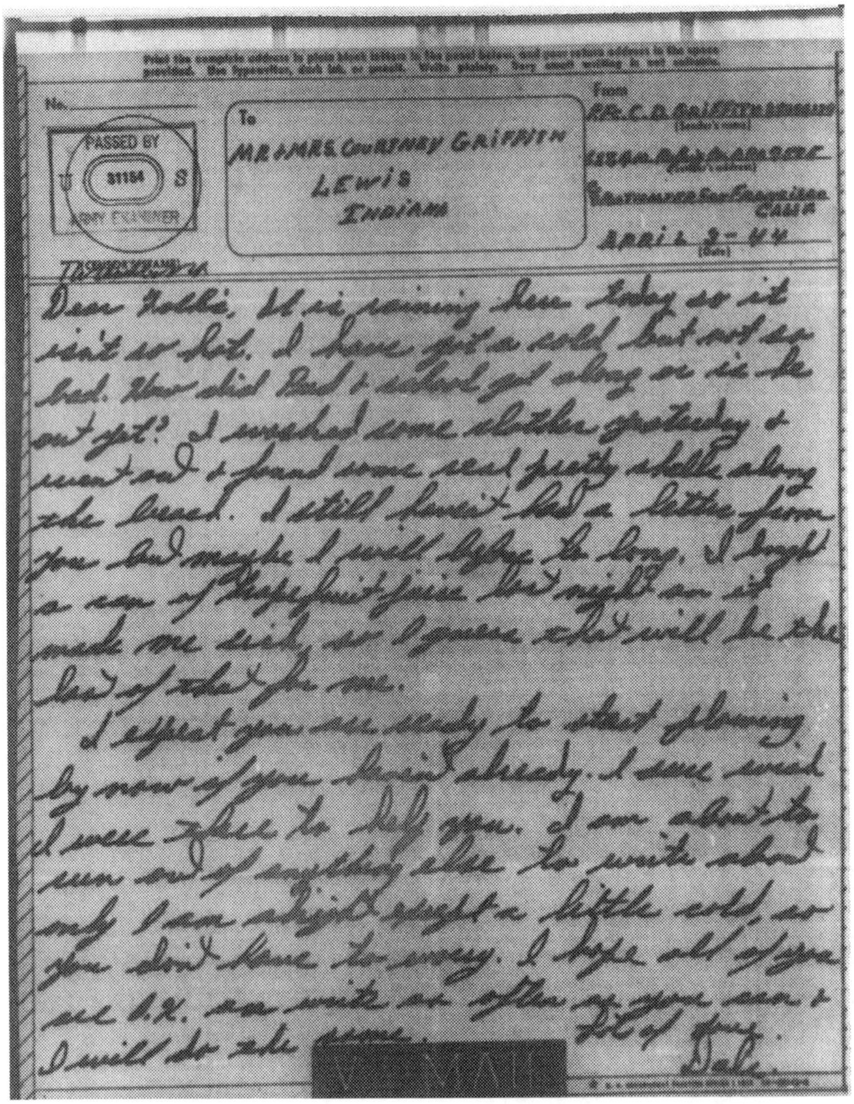

PASSED BY
U 31184 S
ARMY EXAMINER

To
MR & MRS COURTNEY GRIFFITH
LEWIS
INDIANA

From
PFC. C. D. GRIFFITH [illegible]
(Sender's name)
[illegible]
(Sender's address)
[illegible] San Francisco
CALIF
APRIL 3-44
(Date)

Dear Folks, It is raining here today so it isn't so hot. I have got a cold but not so bad. How did Dad & school get along or is he out yet? I washed some clothes yesterday & went out & found some real pretty shells along the beach. I still haven't had a letter from you but maybe I will before so long. I bought a can of grapefruit juice last night an it made me sick, so I guess that will be the last of that for me.

I expect you are ready to start plowing by now if you haven't already. I sure wish I were there to help you. I am about to run out of anything else to write about only I am alright except a little cold, so you don't have to worry. I hope all of you are O.K. so write as often as you can & I will do the same.

Lot of Love,
Dale.

V-MAIL

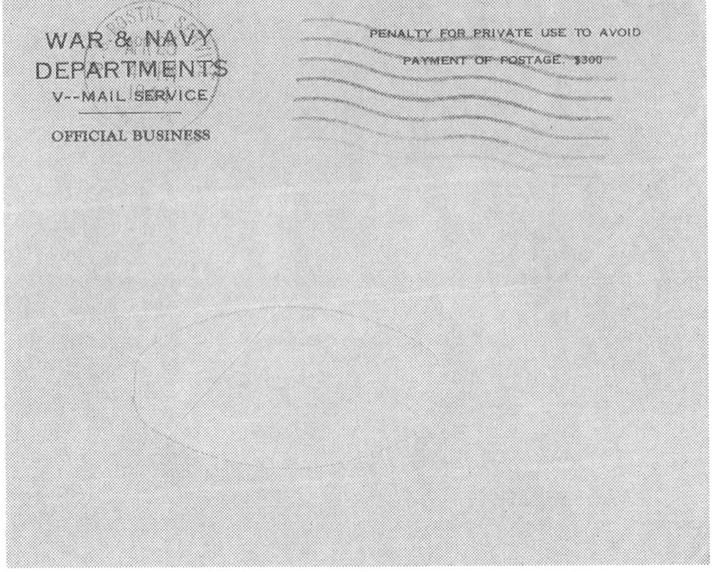

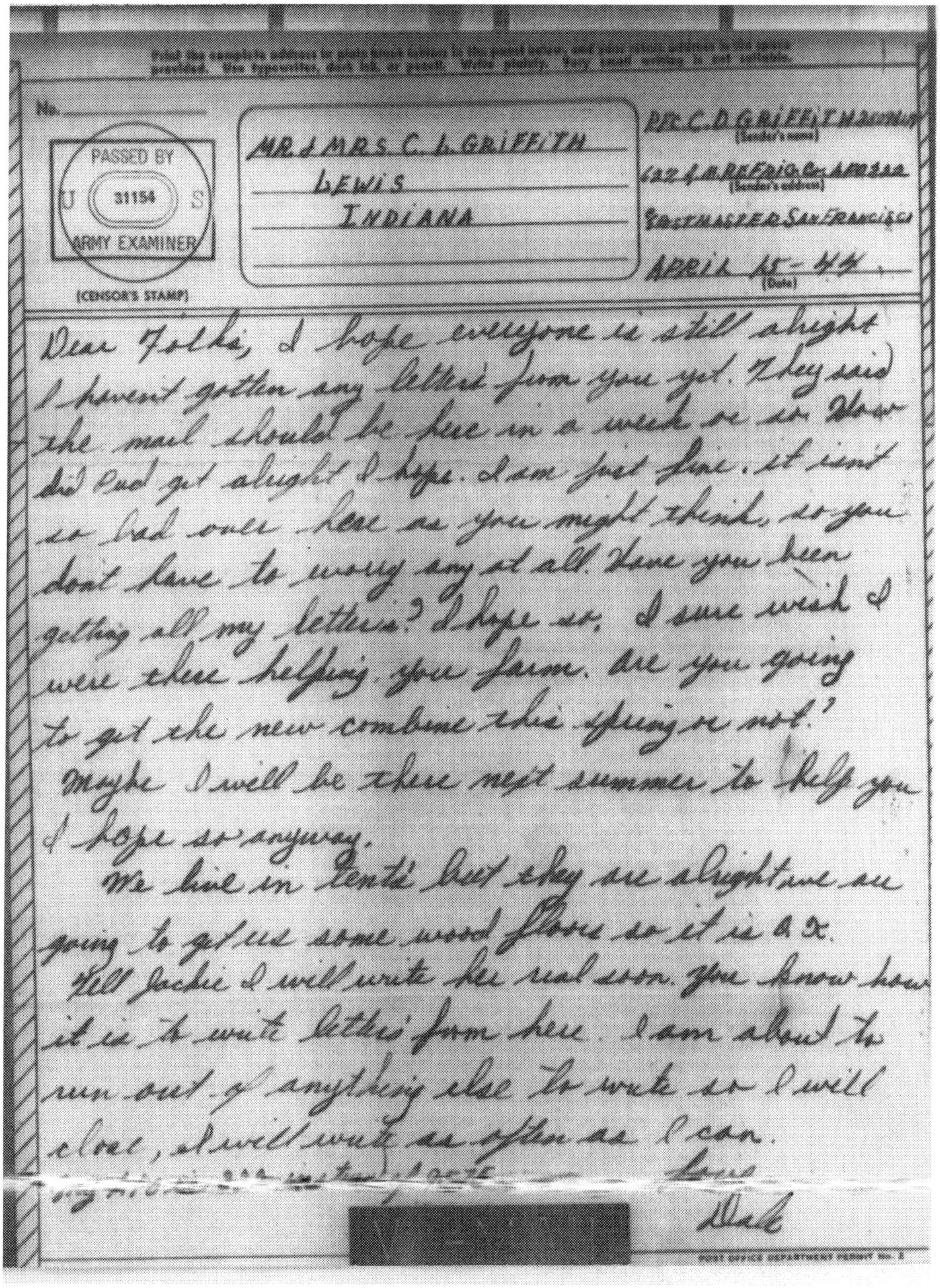

Print the complete address in plain block letters in the panel below, and your return address in the space provided. Use typewriter, dark ink, or pencil. Write plainly. Very small writing is not suitable.

No. ______

PASSED BY
U 31154 S
ARMY EXAMINER
(CENSOR'S STAMP)

MR & MRS. C. L. GRIFFITH
LEWIS
INDIANA

PFC C. D. GRIFFITH [illegible]
(Sender's name)
[illegible] REFRIG. Co. APO [illegible]
(Sender's address)
POSTMASTER SAN FRANCISCO
APRIL 15 - 44.
(Date)

Dear Folks, I hope everyone is still alright
I haven't gotten any letters from you yet. They said
the mail should be here in a week or so. How
did Bud get alright I hope. I am just fine. it isn't
so bad over here as you might think, so you
dont have to worry any at all. Have you been
getting all my letters? I hope so. I sure wish I
were there helping you farm. are you going
to get the new combine this spring or not?
Maybe I will be there next summer to help you
I hope so anyway.
We live in tents but they are alright we are
going to get us some wood floors so it is O.K.
Tell Jackie I will write her real soon. you know how
it is to write letters from here. I am about to
run out of anything else to write so I will
close, I will write as often as I can.
[illegible] Love
Dale

POST OFFICE DEPARTMENT PERMIT No. 2

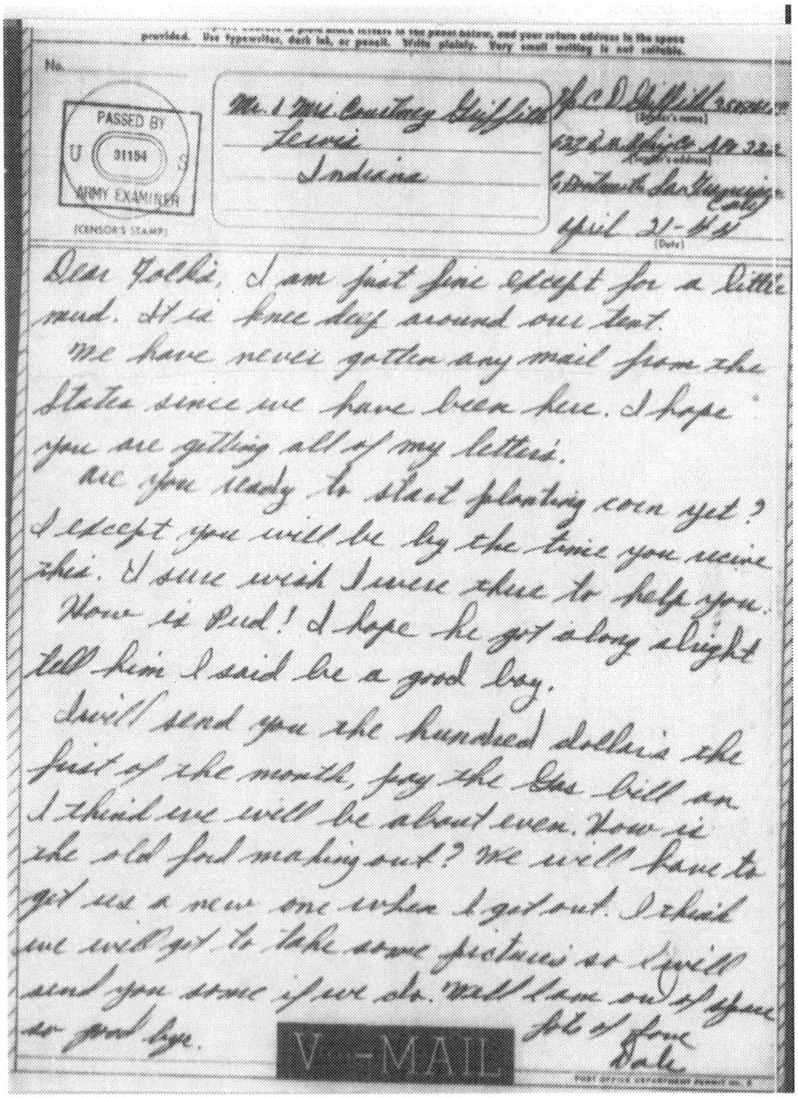

Dear Folks, I am just fine except for a little mud. It is knee deep around our tent.

We have never gotten any mail from the States since we have been here. I hope you are getting all of my letters.

Are you ready to start planting corn yet? I expect you will be by the time you recieve this. I sure wish I were there to help you.

How is Bud! I hope he got along alright tell him I said be a good boy.

I will send you the hundred dollars the first of the month, pay the Gas bill an I think we will be about even. How is the old ford making out? We will have to get us a new one when I get out. I think we will get to take some pictures so I will send you some if we do. Well I am out of space so good bye.

Lots of love
Dale

V--MAIL
POST OFFICE DEPARTMENT PERMIT NO. 2

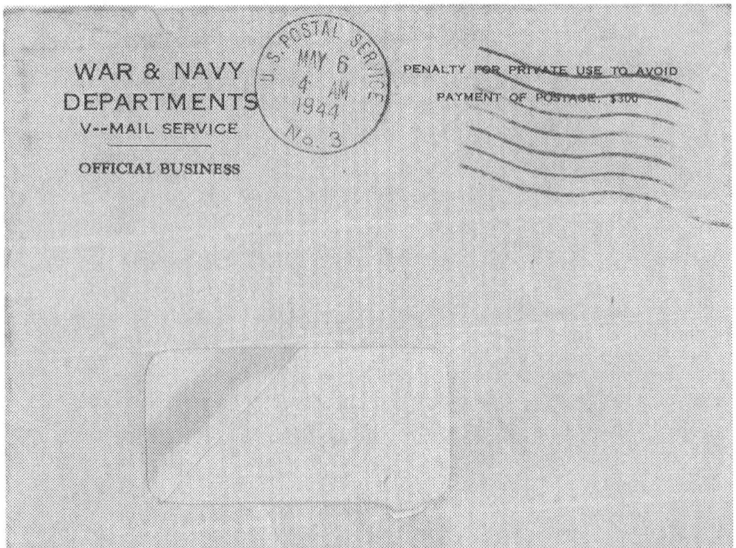

WAR & NAVY DEPARTMENTS
V--MAIL SERVICE
OFFICIAL BUSINESS
U.S. POSTAL SERVICE
MAY 6
4 AM
1944
No. 3
PENALTY FOR PRIVATE USE TO AVOID PAYMENT OF POSTAGE, $300

2 April 27

Dear Folks,

I have been meaning to write for the last three days but seems I never got to. Walter Tennis is here beside of me. He lives about 100 yds. from me. We sure have talked about ever-one we ever knew HAHA. I work from 4 in the evening until 12 at night, so it isn't so bad after all. I got my first mail today, I sure was glad to get it.

2

How is Bud? I expect he will be going fishing ever day from now on. Did I tell you are APO is 322 now. I think I told you once before but for fear you didn't get it I will tell you again. I am going to get me a haircut tomorrow, an wash some clothes. I washed Sun. but I have to wash again. It isn't so bad. But I think I will get some-one to wash for me when I get back.

3

Have you been getting
the 50 bond yet or not?
I hope so. If you ever
need them for anything cash
them in. How is farming?
I expect you are planting
corn by now. I sure
wish I were there to
help you. Maybe I will
be some of these days.
I think I will buy me
a house when I get
there. Tell Jackie I said
hello, an I will write
them as soon as I can.
I got something in my
eye a couple of weeks

4

ago. I had it taken out
day before yesterday. It is
alright now. I am about
to run out of anything
else to write so I better
close. I found out plain
air mail comes as fast
is v mail. Well I must
close. Lots of Love
Dale

May 3-44

Dear Folks,

I have been getting your letter's just fine, I hope you are getting all of mine. It take's about 16 days for your letter's to get here.

It is really raining here to-night. so I guess I won't go over & see Walter.

I haven't got the money order sent out yet, but I will in the next two or three day's

are you done planting corn yet or not? How much did you plant? I sure wish I were there to help you

3

You have been wanting to know what to send me. I would like to have some T shirts size 36 if you find any send them. I don't need any thing else.

Tell Pud to buy him a new suit with the next check you get.

How many war bonds have I got now? maybe I can buy me a house when I get out. at least a new shot gun.

How is Jackie & Bugs? Tell them I said hello. I have about run out & I think Walker is coming up so I will close

Lots of Love
Dad

CLAY CITY JUL 12 1944 IND.

4

May 5-44

Dear Folks;

It is really raining again to-night. It has rained almost every day this week. Walter said he was coming over to-night, I don't expect he will come since it is raining.

I got the money order today so I am sending it, Be sure an tell me if you get it or not. Spend it for anything you need. Are you getting the 50 bonds or not. Be sure an tell me.

I got a letter from you to day written the 19th of april so it takes a little over two weeks for them to get here.

2

I expect you will be done planting corn by the time you get this. How much did you plant this year? It sure seems like it has been a long time since I drove the old tractor, but I believe I can still plow corn if I had too. I burned my finger with a match & it is really hurting, I can't hardly write, maybe it will stop before long.

How is Jackie & Bugs? I have been meaning to write them for the last week, but seems I don't. I work in the day time, & at night I have to wash clothes or something, not that bad but almost. Tomorrow night I think Walter & I will go to the show

3

if it isn't raining, It is about
3 miles to where they have
the show. How is old Rud?
is he helping plow? I bet
he will be next year. I
hope I am there, I think
maybe I stand a pretty good
chance of being there, for
they have got them on
the run now. I was down
at the bakery today & weighted
my self guess how much 160
lbs, I lost about 20 lbs since
I was home. This heat sure
brings it out of you. Dad you
should be here for awhile Ha Ha.
I have about run out of anything to write so I will close
hope all is fine.

Lots of Love
Dale

AMERICAN RED CROSS

Dear Folks May 18-44

I hope you have been getting all of my letters for I try to write as often as I can. I got one letter from you so far this week. I am just fine I hope you are all the same.

I went to the show last night it was pretty good. Have you got all of the corn planted yet or not? I sure wish I were there to help you. Have you ever gotten the money order

"To furnish volunteer aid to the sick and wounded of armies ......" and "To act in matters of voluntary relief and in accord with the military and naval authorities as a medium of communication between the people of the United States of America and their Army and Navy ......" The Charter of The American National Red Cross. By Act of Congress January 5, 1905.

FORM 539 A

AMERICAN RED CROSS

2

I sent you? I hope so & the
Co bonds. If the war last
long enough I may have enough
for that new car HA HA. How
is old Bud? tell him I said
not to catch all the fish out
of the pond. It sure is hot
here, if you get under a cocoanut
tree for shade you will get
hit on the head HA HA. I don't
know if Hank & I will go to
the show tonight or not. I work
in the day time now [illegible]

"To furnish volunteer aid to the sick and wounded of armies ......" and "To act in matters of voluntary relief and in accord with the military and naval authorities as a medium of communication between the people of the United States of America and their Army and Navy ......" The Charter of The American National Red Cross. By Act of Congress January 5, 1905.

FORM 539 A

AMERICAN RED CROSS

3

I can write of a night, which
gives me more time, so I can
keep up now, that is if I get
any letters. I wrote Clint yesterday.
Seems I am about to run out
so I will close. Lots of Love

Dale

"To furnish volunteer aid to the sick and wounded of armies ......" and "To act in matters of voluntary relief and in accord with the military and naval authorities as a medium of communication between the people of the United States of America and their Army and Navy ......" The Charter of The American National Red Cross. By Act of Congress January 5, 1905.

FORM 539 A

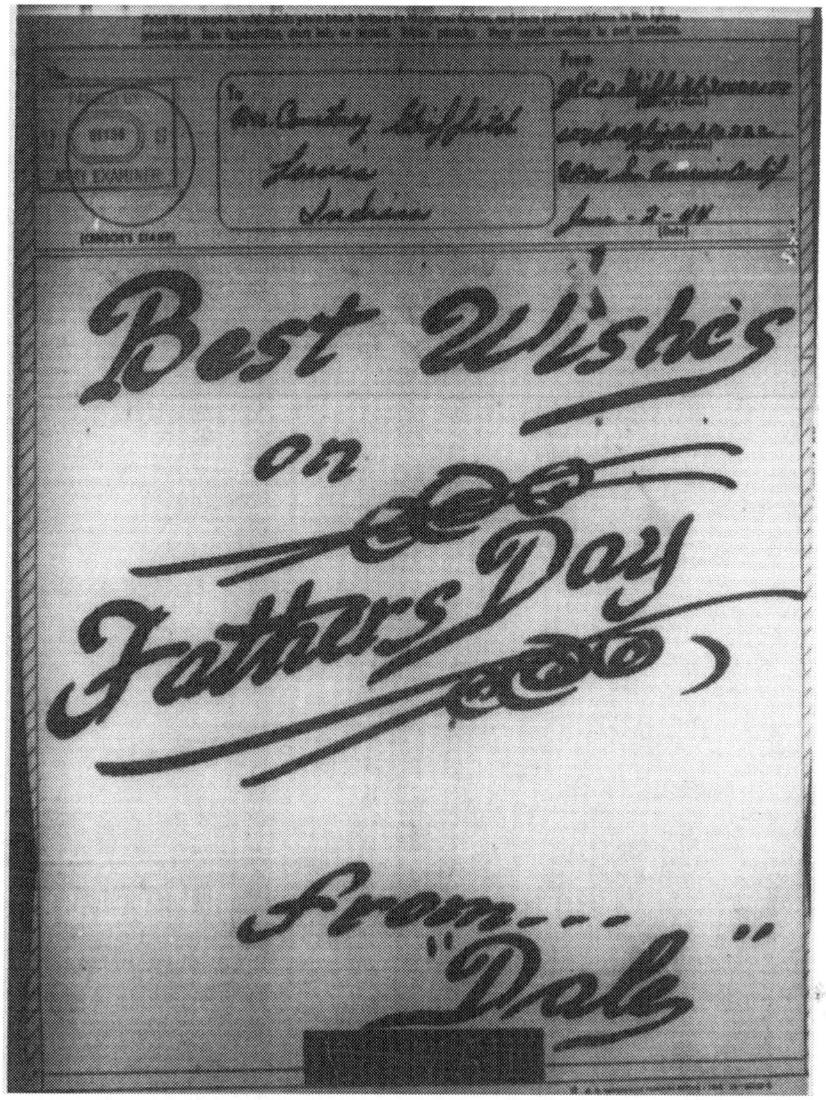
Best Wishes
on
Fathers Day
From....
"Dale"
[redacted]

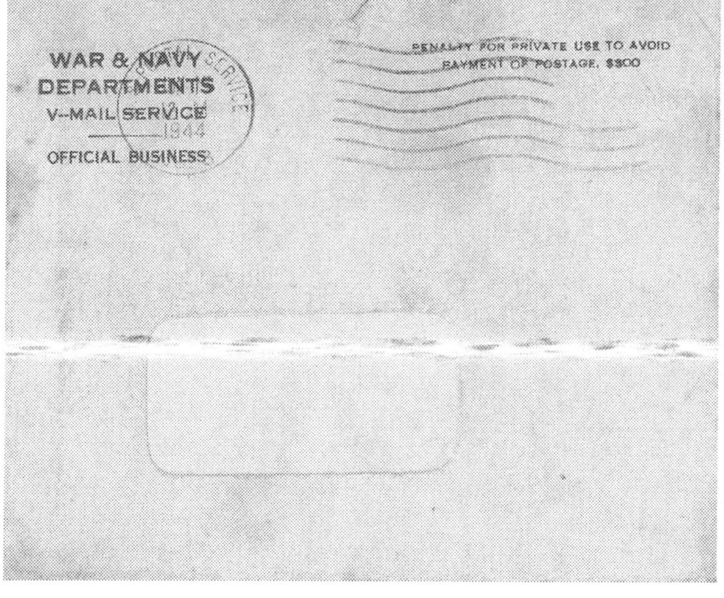
WAR & NAVY
DEPARTMENTS
V--MAIL SERVICE
OFFICIAL BUSINESS
1944
PENALTY FOR PRIVATE USE TO AVOID
PAYMENT OF POSTAGE, $300

Print the complete address in plain block letters in the panel below, and your return address in the space provided. Use typewriter, dark ink, or pencil. Write plainly. Very small writing is not suitable.

No. ______

PASSED BY
U 31154 S
ARMY EXAMINER
(CENSOR'S STAMP)

To
Mr. Mrs. Courtney Griffith
Lewis
Indiana

From
Pfc. C. D. Griffith [illegible]
(Sender's name)
627 Q.M. Ord. Co. APO 322
(Sender's address)
% P.M. San Francisco Calif.
June. 3-44
(Date)

Dear Folks,

Well another day & still no letters from you. I hope everyone is alright. I am just fine. I went swimming this afternoon.

I built me a chair to night. so I am all fixed up now. It is hard for me to write, since I haven't heard from you for so long. I hope you are doing farming by the time you get this you should be. How many fish have you caught dad. Did you ever use the rods or not. If you were here you could really catch some. When I get home we will go to Mich. an stay a week. I know you would like that. I have ran out of any-thing else to write so I must close. I hope you are getting my mail & I start getting some.

Lots of Love Dale

V---MAIL

U.S. GOVERNMENT PRINTING OFFICE: 1943 [illegible]

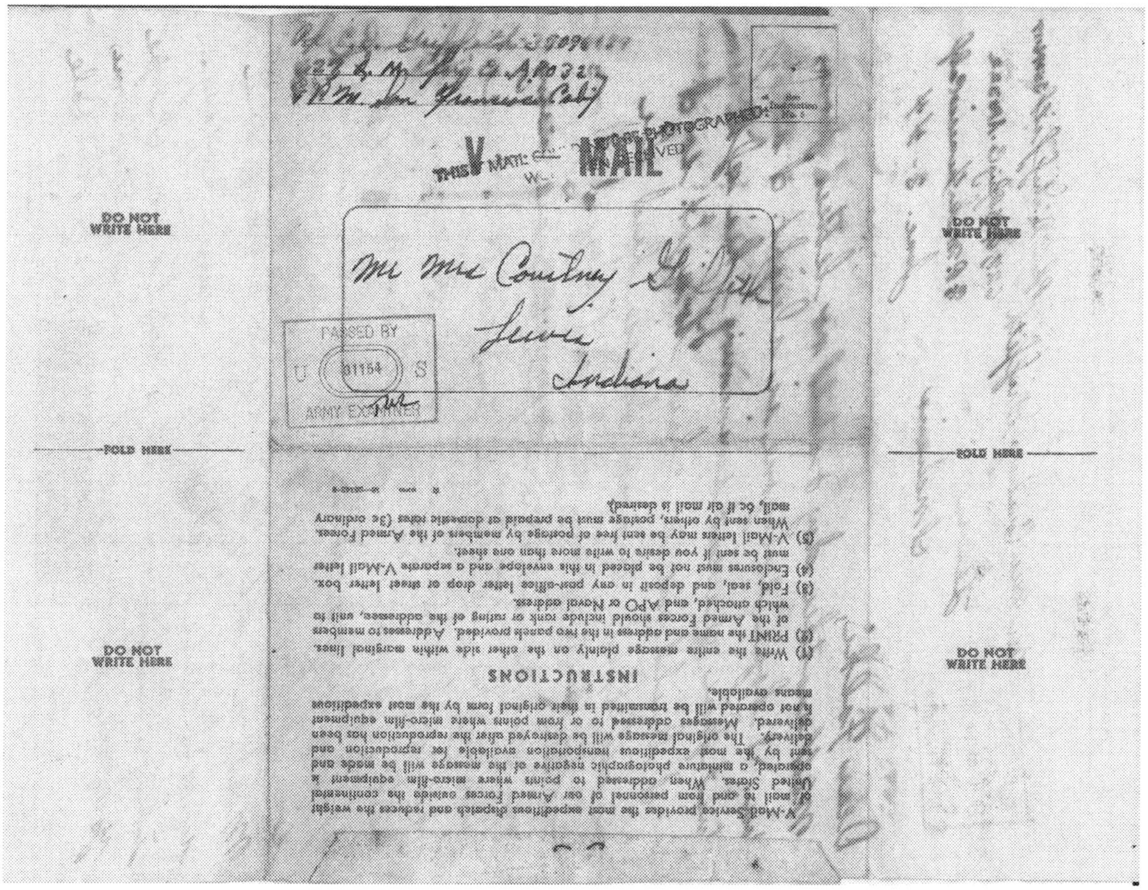
THIS V MAIL
PHOTOGRAPHED
DO NOT WRITE HERE
Mr Mrs Courtney
Lewis
Indiana
PASSED BY
U.S.
ARMY EXAMINER
FOLD HERE
DO NOT WRITE HERE

June 7-44

Dear Folks,

I didn't get a letter from you today. I hope everyone is alright. I really have a headache to-night. I have had it almost every day since I been here. I sure hope it gets better soon.

They sure are giving it to the Germans now aren't they. I expect the Japs will get the same thing before long.

We haven't any lights to-night only a candle so I am going to hurry up & get this written before dark.

For supper we had steak potatoes peas & cake. so we aren't going hungry HaHa.

2)

I wrote Clint a letter last night. I got one from him day before yesterday. How is Pud on the pony. I can see him riding her. He will have to get a cart for her. I hope the corn is big enough to plow & it isn't raining to often. I have to write aunt Marie & Uncle Ray real soon I got a letter from them that was 3 mo's old. I don't know what was wrong. We even got letters from much yet. I must close I'll write tomorrow

Lots of Love

Dal

P.S. Give Pud the penny HaHa.

Sun. July 2-44

Dear Folks,

I rec. a v-mail from you today. It is the first letter I have had for five days.

Walter has been up for the last three hrs. We have been playing cards. We went swimming this afternoon.

I got a letter from Clint today. said he thought he would get out of the hospital before long.

Where are you going the 4th. You should take Pud to Terre Haute. Maybe me & him can go next year.

The war news is really good now. Lif mag. from now things should be really going our way.

2

I wrote Aunt Marie a letter
last night. I have gotten 7
letters from her in the
last week. I told Unk Ray I
might need a job in the
new mine.

Do you remember that girl
Charlie J. used to go with?
she has been writing me
almost every day. I almost
have to answer them. I guess
she thinks she has got
me hooked.

I hope the farming is
about over with. It won't
be long until time to kill
red tails. How many have
you killed? I know this is
very short but must close. Hope
all is well. I am just fine

Lots of Love
Dale

July 9-44

Dear Folks;

I rec. seven letters from you today. They are the first I have had for a long time.

I hope you got the corn picker in one of your letters you said you thought you could get one from Ollie.

I'm sending you some pictures they aren't very clear but maybe you can see them.

Looks like the clothes could stand a little washing or something Ha Ha.

Tell Paul, I got his letter today. I will send him $25 next month to start school on.

I got a letter from Jackie. I will have to

2

ans. it to-night.

We had steaks for dinner & supper today. We are getting as good a meals here as we did back in the states.

How many fish fries have you had? Or are the fish biting?

I don't want you to worry when you don't hear from me for the mail doesn't get here either. I'm over the headache now.

I am going to the show to-night so I must close.

Lots of Love

Carl

Aug. 3-44

Dear Folks,

I rec. four letters from you yesterday, they were the first I have had for a month.

I'm just fine & hope all of you are the same.

There was an australian here today he was selling whisky for \$38.40 a quart did you ever hear anything like that? (We) told him to go on.

They are taking pictures now I'm going to have mine taken to-night I will send it to you as soon as it's developed.

I haven't gotten those you were going to send me. [redacted]

2

I got a letter from Billy yesterday so I'm going to write him. Then go down & see Walter.

Have you ever gotten those native pictures I send you? I will send you some more one of these days.

How is Bud? Are you going to get him a buggy for his pony? We can take his girl a ride when he gets it.

I have my air plane made I'll send it next week it really looks nice believe it or not. I'm going to make a letter opener some time this week.

I could of sold the plane

for #6 as you know it
is O.K. Ha.
I got a letter from
Jackie yesterday, so I
will have to ans. it.
She said Terry had really
grown, told me about
the fish fry. I wish I
had of been there.
I cant think of anything
else to write so I will
close. Lots of Love
Dad

Vol. 2. No. 354. AMERICAN EDITION Monday, November 6, 1944.

GUINEA GOLD

RED ARMY REACHES BUDAPEST

DESPERATE BATTLE FOR CITY EXPECTED

LONDON, Sun.: Powerful tank columns of Marshal Malinovsky's Second Ukrainian Army have forced their way to the gates of Budapest, capital of Hungary and richest prize of the Soviet High Command's central European campaign.

Moscow's latest communique placed the Russians within nine miles of the city, but Moscow radio announced that Soviet armored formations, with air support, had broken into the outskirts of Budapest.

MOSCOW radio added that one Soviet column yesterday captured a railway junction two miles from Budapest and so cut one of the escape routes for the German garrison inside the city. Scores of low-flying fighters and fighter-bombers were blasting enemy entrenchments on the immediate outskirts of the capital from which refugees were fleeing in increasing numbers.

Refugees who reached the Russian lines yesterday said the Germans were massing equipment on

ENEMY MASSES EQUIPMENT . . .

a vast scale for a last desperate attempt to stem the Soviet offensive, while buildings inside Budapest were being heavily fortified.

Last night's correspondents' dispatches from Moscow stated that newly arrived enemy reserves, rushed up to delay the Soviet advance, were being smashed and captured so rapidly that they were "practically stepping straight from German trains into Russian prison camps."

Those Hungarians remaining in Budapest, following the German refusal to declare the capital an

HUNGARIANS IN REVOLT . . .

open city, continued yesterday to wage open warfare against the enemy.

Ankara radio reported to-day that Partisan forces were in control of the industrial area of Budapest, which on Friday came under Russian artillery fire.

Military commentators in London pointed out that if the Germans were forced to withdraw from Budapest, the Hungarian Army would be isolated in the north-eastern hilly part of Hungary, containing only a scattered assortment of small settlements and villages. Loss of this army to the Germans would be a serious blow, they said, because despite heavy punishment suffered during its long retreat it remained a valuable asset to the Nazis.

In the other active sector of the Eastern Front, Soviet troops penetrating into south-eastern East Prussia were reported last night to have repulsed a series of fierce German counter-attacks. Heavy snow restricted large-scale operations in this area.

WOUNDED DOCTOR MAY SURVIVE

SYDNEY, Sun.: The prospects of recovery for Dr. Reginald Stewart Jones, who was shot in an affray at Maroubra last week, were reported brighter by officials of St. Vincent's Hospital last night. They said that he now had a fifty-fifty chance of living.

Large crowds gathered outside the hospital last night to read the latest bulletins on the doctor's condition, while offers of blood for transfusion purposes poured in from Australian and Allied servicemen. Offers were telegraphed from as far afield as New Guinea and W.A.

BUSY WEEK AHEAD IN FEDERAL POLITICS

CANBERRA, Sun.: With the next Federal Parliamentary session less than two weeks off, the tempo of events here will increase this week.

War Cabinet is to meet on Wednesday, the War Advisory Council on Thursday, and full Cabinet on Friday. The Production Executive also will meet during the week. The House of Representatives will meet on Wednesday week and the Senate a week later. It is expected that there will be a secret sitting of both Houses to discuss such matters as relief for war-torn countries.

Swedes Kill Nazis

LONDON, Sun.: German troops withdrawing from Northern Finland into Norway along the road running parallel to the Swedish frontier were fired on yesterday by Swedish Army patrols, who alleged that the Nazis had violated Swiss neutrality. Several Germans were killed.

Franco Says He Is Lilywhite Neutral

LONDON, Sun.: Spain never had allied herself with the Axis and its regime, and, in reality, was a democratic one, General Francisco Franco declared in an interview with the British United Press correspondent at Madrid.

The Spanish dictator admitted that this statement would cause some surprise, but he said his Government's policy was animated by the "purest Christian principles."

Franco stated that Spain always had maintained neutrality, but within a few minutes he defended his action in sending the Spanish Blue Division to fight alongside the Germans in earlier battles in Russia.

●THEY CAME TO CONQUER: Dead German soldiers lie alongside their wrecked armor along a road in Western Europe. They were blasted from the air and the ground as they retreated from the Allies. (USOWI picture.)

5000 R.A.F. & U.S. PLANES BLAST NAZI INDUSTRIES

LONDON, Sun.: Six great Allied armadas, totalling upwards of 5000 RAF and US planes, yesterday gave Germany's synthetic oil, aircraft production and railway centres a terrific two-way hammering.

FOUR thousand bombers and fighters hit Germany from the west, while 500 US Fortresses and Liberators, escorted by 400 fighters, flew deep into the Reich from bases in Italy.

At least 1300 Fortresses and Liberators of the Eighth USAAF in Britain, covered by swarms of American fighters, attacked objectives in the Hamburg and Harburg areas; at Misburg, near Hanover; a synthetic oil plant at Gelsenkirchen, and railway yards at Saarbrucken. RAF Lancasters, meanwhile, struck at aircraft factories in the Solingen area, south of the Ruhr.

Targets for the Italian-based heavy bombers were in the industrial areas of Coblenz, Regensburg, and Augsburg.

Allied losses in the day's offensive from Britain were eight bombers and six fighters.

100,000 Tons Of H.E. On Reich In Month

LONDON, Sun.: In a record month of activity in October, British and American planes from Britain unloaded more than 100,000 tons of high explosives on

The Minister for Air (Sir Archibald Sinclair) said today that the greater part of this bombload was carried by British night bombers.

DESPERATE BUT FUTILE ENEMY BID TO WIN AIR SUPREMACY OVER LEYTE

LEYTE Is., Sun.: The Japanese are throwing in all their available air forces in an all-out bid to wrest air supremacy in the central Philippines from the Americans, but so far with little or no result. A CBS correspondent suggests that the enemy has called on his best fliers to match veteran US pilots.

FLYING from groups of airfields on Luzon, Cebu, Mindanao, and Mindoro, Japanese formations—as many as 100 aircraft at a time—are persistently attempting to break through the Allied air umbrella over Leyte. The CBS correspondent says, however, that he has never seen more than 12 of the enemy planes reach vital areas behind the American lines at any one time, and these usually have been shot down down or driven off before they have had a chance to do any damage.

Another Press correspondent yesterday saw a group of 75 enemy planes covering a convoy off Ormoc Bay, on the western coast [illegible] them in a battle lasting several hours. No US fighters were lost.

Other Press dispatches state that it now has become a race between American engineers rushing the construction of new airfields to enable more fighter planes to go into action, and the ability of the Japanese to organise bigger raids with the hope of smashing through Allied protective air cover.

Besides covering US ground troops on Leyte, Allied patrol planes are continuing their widespread attacks in support of operations generally. In the latest series of raids they derailed an enemy supply train on Luzon Island, destroyed five parked planes on Cebu, and bombed airfields on [illegible]

HARD LAND BATTLE

LEYTE Is., Sun.: American forces are engaged in bloody local battles with reinforced Japanese troops trying to break out of the restricted area they hold around Ormoc Bay, on the western coast of Leyte Island. So far all enemy attempts have failed.

NEW WAR CABINET OF PHILIPPINES MEETS

LEYTE IS., Sun.: The War Cabinet of President Osmena's Philippines Govt. held its first meeting at Tacloban yesterday.

Immediate decisions were made [illegible]

—S-E ASIA BATTLES—

Japs In Suburbs Of Kweilin Base

CHUNGKING, Sun.: Japanese columns have penetrated into the suburbs of Kweilin, American air base and capital of Kwangsi Province, on three sides, and are advancing slowly against stubborn Chinese resistance.

Another Japanese column has by-passed Kweilin from the east and is now advancing down the railway line towards the American air base at Liuchow, which is already menaced by another [illegible]

Allied Gains In Western Burma

KANDY (Ceylon), Sun.: Indian troops in Western Burma have captured more strongly fortified Japanese positions on the hills commanding the strategic highway between Tiddim and Fort White.

On the Arakan front, West African troops have captured several villages north of Buthedaung, and are maintaining contact with Japanese rearguards. Fighters and fighter-bombers [illegible]

ROOSEVELT MAY HAVE TO WORK WITH HOSTILE CONGRESS IF RETURNED; KEEN ELECTION FINISH IS EXPECTED

NEW YORK, Sun.: Close voting is expected in Thursday's presidential election. Public opinion polls indicate that if President Roosevelt is re-elected, he may face a hostile congress.

IF the popular vote is overwhelmingly in his favor, President Roosevelt can confront Congress with the claim that he represents the people's will.

He tacitly recognised this when he declared that he would rather be defeated by a large vote than elected by a small one.

Unless all the public opinion polls and "straw" votes are misleading, the election will be decided by the industrial States of New York, Pennsylvania, New Jersey, and Massachusetts, with New York and Pennsylvania as the final battleground.

Correspondents say the President has shown skill in belittling Gov. Dewey's importance without even mentioning his name. Some say he has been helped by Dewey's own reliance upon distortion, "which, however effective in winning rank and file votes, has not earned him a reputation for honesty even among Republicans."

The more sober columnists of both parties deplore the low standard of electioneering argument.

Walter Lippmann says that it is "repulsive in its irrelevancies and callous unawareness of the great matters of life and death which the American people are being called on to decide."

Other leading commentators claim that were Gov. Dewey a man of Wendell Willkie's stature, his victory would be certain, for the country is weary of the present Administration and would welcome a change.

However, they say, thousands who are luke-warm about Roosevelt, fear to hand over the Government at such a critical time to a young man of unsettled convictions and limited experience.

HIGHLIGHTS OF SPORTING NEWS.

●FOOTBALL: Army replaced Notre Dame as the top-ranking football team in the nation, according to the weekly Associated Press poll. Irish had led 14 straight weeks. The top 10 in order are: Army, Notre Dame, Ohio State, Randolph Field, Georgia Tech, Navy, Iowa Pre-flight, North Carolina Preflight, Illinois, and Michigan.

Ed Kubale and Frank Bridges, assistant coaches of Texas Tigers, have begun duty as joint coaches for the remainder of the season, following the resignation of Pete Cawthorn. Kubale coached Centre College and Bridges at at Baylor University.

●BASEBALL: Tom Sheehan resigned as the Boston Braves coach today, and Del Bissonette, who managed the Braves' Hartford Eastern League Farm team last year, was signed immediately to replace him. Sheehan, who pitched in both major leagues and was a veteran minor league manager, was the Braves coach for the past five years. Bissonette, his successor, played first base for Brooklyn Dodgers 15 yrs. ago.

Southern Association voted today to reinstate the Shaughnessy play-off system for next season. Southern Association has played the split season for the past two years, with the winners of each half playing a seven-game series for the championship. The directors tentatively set April 27 as the opening date and September 9 as closing date of the 1945 season.

The major league war relief games poured more than 300,000 dol. into the treasury of the National War Fund and American Red Cross, it was revealed by the Office of Baseball Commissioner Landis. The total was 329,555 dol., which was divided evenly between two war agencies.

●BOXING: The bout between Luther ("Slugger") White, Baltimore negro, and Willie Royce, scheduled for San Francisco, has been cancelled by the State Athletic Commission following the report of a boxing inspector that White has a glass eye. In Los Angeles, Willie Ritchie, a lightweight champion of 30 years ago, now chief boxing inspector, said he learned that White's eye was removed in Baltimore a year ago, following a fight with Sammy Angott in that city. He added that White was passed for his first fight with Henry Armstrong in California last July, but the examining physician at that time recommended a re-examination of White's eye before any subsequent bout.

●ATHLETICS: Dan Ferris, secretary-treasurer of the National Amateur Athletic Association, received word today that Gundar Hagg and Arne Andersson, Swedish track stars, had declined the invitation to visit the United States during the indoor track season.

The message from the Swedish Amateur Athletic Association gave no reason, but said a letter of explanation would follow. "That is a disappointment to all track fans in the United States," said Ferris, "but I have not given up. I am going to try once more to persuade them to come over and compete this winter."

THANKSGIVING DINNERS FOR THE ARMED FORCES

CHICAGO, Sun.: More than 95 per cent. of all personnel in the armed forces, including those held by the enemy, will get an old-fashioned Thanksgiving Dinner November 23. This was disclosed today by Col. H. R. McKenzie, of the Office of Quartermaster-General.

The Red Cross is taking steps to get processed turkey to prisoners in Germany and Japan, while elsewhere service men and women will consume 90,000,000lb. of the holiday bird, including 8,000,000 drumsticks, with all trimmings.

U.S. ONLY NATION READY FOR POST-WAR AVIATION

NEW YORK, Sun.: The United States is the only nation which technically and financially is capable of immediate civil aviation extension. This is being pointed out by the American delegates to the International Air Conference in Chicago.

"THE United States," the "New York Times" correspondent says, "will be able to fly a big four-engine plane across the Atlantic every 15 minutes the moment the war emergency ends.

"On the other hand, the British, who insist that such competition would be ruinous to all other transport in the world, favor international control of aviation."

In a message to the conference, President Roosevelt said he did not believe that the world could wait for several years for air communications.

PREDICTS MAMMOTH POST-WAR AIR-FLEET

WASHINGTON, Sun.: Brookings Institution has released a survey forecasting the development of a vast post-war commercial air fleet, capable of carrying 4,000,000 United States passengers overseas annually, at an ultimate rate of 5 cents per mile. Aviation expert Dr. J. Parker van Zandt, who conducted the survey, said that improvements and volume operations would create "a very large potential air travel market among Americans of moderate income, whose interest in foreign lands has been stimulated by the war."

Marriage Drop In Cities Continues

WASHINGTON, Sun.: There have been fewer marriages this year than last—in the larger cities at least—the Census Bureau reported to-day. A total of 47,889 licenses were issued in the cities with more than 100,000 population in September, compared with 48,009 in the same month last year.

NEW FOUR-PROCESS RIVETING MACHINE

BUFFALO (NY), Sun.: The General Engineering Company's Buffalo plant has developed a four-process riveting machine, which it is believed will save 2000 manhours in building an airplane.

Howard C. Abt, Assistant Plant General Manager said last night that the machine would put a rivet through metal up to three-eighths of an inch thick. It performed four operations which were formerly done separately: drilling, counter-sinking, placing and heading the rivets.

NAVY'S BIG SMOKE

OAKLAND, Sun.: More than 8,000,000 cigars a month are shipped to American blue-jackets in the Pacific, but the demand is for 20,000,000, Navy Supply Depot disclosed here. About 22,000,000 packets of cigarettes also go out each month to navy men afloat and at advanced Pacific bases. They also use 25,000,000 candy bars every thirty days.

Planes From 10-dol. Up At First Defense Sale

DAYTON, Sun.: Prices ranged from 10-dol. to 7500-dol. when officials of the Defense Plant Corporation conducted its first public auction of surplus airplanes at Patterson Field. Nearly 1000 buyers entered bids for nearly half of the 160 planes in the first day of the sale.

A battered Aeronca trainer went for 10-dol. and the day's top price of 7500-dol. was brought by a twin-engined Beechcraft. All planes sold were trainers no longer needed by the USAAF.

Roosevelts May Have Been In Naval Battle

WASHINGTON, Sun.: Mrs. Franklin D. Roosevelt said at a Press Conference Saturday she did not know whether any of her three sons in the Pacific Theatre had been in the Philippines fighting.

She added, however, that John was serving on an aircraft carrier and has been on duty under Admiral William Halsey, Jr., Commander of the Third Fleet, for more than six months.

Marine Colonel James Roosevelt and Lt.-Commander Franklin Roosevelt were also in the Pacific Theater, a fourth son, Col. Elliot Roosevelt was serving in the European theater.

974 JAP. VESSELS HIT BY U.S. SUBS.

WASHINGTON, Sun.: United States submarines operating against the enemy's Pacific supply lines have now sunk, probably sunk, or damaged 974 Japanese ships, the Navy Department announces.

This was disclosed in a statement which reported successful attacks on another 18 enemy vessels. One of the submarines' victims was a destroyer.

Officer Acquitted Of Wife-Killing Charge

CINCINNATI, Sun.: The jury, which deliberated for 101 hours, acquitted Capt. Robert J. Connors, 27, of Philadelphia, of the bathtub death of his pretty wife, Lois, in their hotel room last July.

Prosecution witnesses testified that Mrs. Connors' death resulted from a fractured larynx and shock, caused by violence, but Connors said he had awakened to find his wife's nude body partly submerged in the bathtub. Capt. Connors is a former Fort Knox tank officer.

CONGRESSIONAL MEDAL FOR ANZIO GALLANTRY

WASHINGTON, Sun.: The Congressional Medal of Honor has been awarded to Pvt. James H. Mills, of Fort Meade, Florida, for conspicuous daring in May, near Cisterna, on the Anzio beachhead, Italy.

Single handed, Pvt. Mills killed four Germans and captured nine. By a ruse, he also attracted the enemy's fire to himself and enabled his platoon to capture an enemy strongpoint and take 22 prisoners.

NEWS FROM HOME

●*COLD:* New York temperature hovered in the forties and fifties all Saturday, after dropping to 35deg. during the night.

●*JUDGE:* Judge Charles H. Darling, former Assistant Secretary of the Navy under President Theodore Roosevelt, and recognised as the dean of the legal profession in Vermont, died yesterday at Mary Fletcher Hospital. He was 85.

●*ELECTION:* Registration throughout the nation has been heavy, 13 large cities already having set records. Industrial centers report war workers rushing to qualify. The surge of last-minute registrations in Detroit smashed all records, and neighboring Ohio reports that the total vote is sure to exceed 3,000,000.

●*BIRTHDAY:* The veteran novelist Gertrude Atherton celebrated her 87th birthday today. She has just finished one book and has started on another.

Reforestation Advocated By President

CLARKSBURG (W.V.), Sun.: More than 10,000 persons crowded the station yard here Wednesday to greet President Roosevelt's campaign train returning to Washington from Chicago. The President spoke for 15 minutes on the need of reforestation in the mining regions. "I know we cannot replace coal," he said, "but trees are something we can replace. We have to think in terms of a long crop, something that takes years to grow, but which eventually will be an asset for our grandchildren."

Famous Art Works For California University

LOS ANGELES, Sun.: The famed Arensberg collection, a group of 800 pieces of painting, sculpture, and other art objects acquired by Mr. and Mrs. Walter C. Arensberg, of Hollywood, over 30 years is being donated to Los Angeles campus of the University of California.

The collection includes examples of modern art by Cezanne, Matisse, Picasso, Braque, Leger, Duchamp, Rousseau, Dali and Rivera.

Caesarean Operation Results In Birth Of Quadruplets

NEW YORK, Sun.: The first Caesarean operation for quadruplets was performed successfully in Philadelphia during the week.

AFTER having been treated with a spinal anaesthetic, Mrs. Joseph Ciminelly gave birth to three boys and a girl. All the babies are well and healthy, and are likely to survive. Their average weight is just under 4lb.

Said the obstetrician: "I have never seen so many hands and feet in my life."

At the same time in Chicago, Mrs. Joseph Dieling was happily cuddling her 11th baby, which is of good weight and healthy. Over the past 17 years, Mrs. Dieling has lost 10 children at birth.

Whisky Season Ends

WASHINGTON, Sun.: September whisky production was 365,147 gallons of alcohol, the tax unit said today. This constituted the completion of the whisky operations authorized during August. When the whisky ban was lifted for a one month only August output was 12,581,910 gallons.

LARGE FEET SAVE PARACHUTING PILOT

WASHINGTON, Sun.: Ensign Carl E. Smith, of Houston, Texas, has his large feet to thank for saving his life during a mission over Japanese territory in his fighter.

Ensign Smith was unable to land, or even release his bomb, because of damage to his plane. He climbed to 5000ft. and bailed out. He waited for the customary jerk, but it came from an unorthodox direction, with the result that Smith found himself dangling head down. The harness had been yanked off his shoulders, and "miraculously caught my large brogans." He managed to gain a hold on the harness, and finally hit the water in a sitting position. A destroyer picked him up.

Maine Launches Second Belgian Liberty Ship

SOUTH PORTLAND (Me.), Sun.: The Liberty ship, Belgian Unity, the second to be built by the New England Shipbuilding Corp. for the Belgian Government, went down the ways today. Charles Hallaert, Consul-General at New York, represented the Belgian Government at the ceremony which was broadcast by shortwave to Belgium.

JAPAN "HOPES FOR NEGOTIATED PEACE, PLANS TO KEEP 'INNER GROUP' IN POWER"

NEW YORK, Sun.: There are indications that Japan has not abandoned plans for an eventual negotiated peace, says the "New York Times'" correspondent Frank L. Kluckhohn.

"JAPANESE officers at Tacloban told the locals that Americans were 'softies,' and were so gullible that either Japan or individual Japanese soldiers could surrender at any time and be assured of generous terms," he declared.

"It is said that this view accurately represents the opinion among the enemy's 16 divisions that fought in China and Bataan, and probably comes close to reflecting the general opinion throughout Japan.

"Japanese leaders appear still to be trying to win a negotiated peace in China and some agreement with Russia.

"There is reason to think that the Japanese hope that even the occupation of Japan can be beaten by convincing the American public that the war lords alone were responsible for the war."

Kluckhohn adds that there is evidence that the Japanese are planning to meet occupation not with guerrilla fighting but with a smiling face and friendly hospitality, so that they may be able to re-establish Japan along lines essential to the control of the country by the inner ruling group, with the military clique, at least ostensibly, eliminated.

DIVORCE BILL CRITICISM

LONDON, Sun.: The new Divorce Bill was criticised in the House of Commons on Friday. There was much discussion on a provision enabling an Englishwoman married to an Allied soldier to petition for a divorce at any time.

It was stated that she could marry and divorce three Poles or Americans in three years, while an Englishwoman married to an Englishman must wait three years before petitioning.

"Billy" Reaches Darwin

DARWIN, Sun.: Fresh, agile, and full of enthusiasm, despite his 80 years, Mr. W. M. Hughes, M.H.R., has arrived in Darwin after a journey from Sydney by plane and car. He slept soundly last night through the wildest tropical storm this season. It is expected that he will have travelled 8000 miles by the time he returns to Sydney.

Eire Servicemen's Seven V.C's

LONDON, Sat.: Seven Victoria Crosses had been won by natives of Eire in this war up to last February, states a correspondent of "The Times."

"Eire contains few factors threatening the possibility of a better understanding with Britain," he declares.

"Thanks to British wisdom and forbearance, old suspicions are dying by degrees. Anti-British sentiment will last as long as those still cherishing it, but its fires surely lack fuel.

"There is no obvious reason why Eire should not in future, after due negotiation, and greatly to the common advantage, provide Britain with one of her much needed export markets.

TRAGIC PLIGHT OF DUTCH CHILDREN UNDER NAZI HEEL

LONDON, Sun.: Shocking malnutrition among Dutch children is revealed by "The Times" correspondent at South Beveland.

"It is bitterly cold, and only the strongest children have the strength to run around," says the correspondent. "The lucky ones among these children, who formerly were perhaps the best cared for in Europe, wear wooden shoes. Others have bundles of soaking wet rags wrapped round their feet.

"A colleague of mine who was in Russia says he never saw such malnutrition among Russian children as is shown by these Dutch boys and girls, who are also dirty because there is no soap.

"It is the worst bit of liberated Europe I have seen."

Election In Britain When Germany Is Defeated

LONDON, Sun.: The National Government will continue only until Germany has been defeated. Then, regardless of the position in the Pacific war, a general election will be held on party lines.

That is clear from a speech by Mr. Churchill during the week in the House of Commons and the subsequent debate, when a Bill to extend the life of Parliament for 12 months was passed.

Political correspondents say the election is likely to take place next summer.

WOOL DEFICIT SUBSIDY

ANY deficit existing at the end of the wool purchase arrangement, and representing the difference between prices paid by Australian manufacturers and the flat-rate value of wool purchased by them, will be met by a Commonwealth subsidy.

An assurance to this effect has been given by the Federal Treasurer (Mr. Chifley) to the Commerce Minister (Mr. Scully).

WORLD NEWS IN BRIEF

AIDED GERMANS: Chastenant Depuysseur, 73, who described himself as a count, was condemned to death by the Paris Assize Court for having aided the Germans. He admitted that he had sent hundreds of letters to French people, attacking Britain, the Jews, and de Gaulle, and praising Germany.

GERMANY-JAPAN AIR LINK: Stockholm messages state that the Germans are organising a non-stop air service between Germany and Japan. Giant six-engined Junkers 390, Junkers 90 four-engined Messerschmitts and Heinkels, and six-engined Focke-Wulfs will be used.

FLIERS AS FARMERS

AUSTRALIAN fliers, on their way home from the European war zone, are working on farms in America while awaiting travel orders. They are paid up to 4 dollars (£1/4/-) a day, plus board and lodging.

CHETNICK TREACHERY: The free Yugoslav radio says that General Mikhailovitch's son and daughter have joined the forces of the Yugoslav President (Marshal Tito) to "efface the shame of their father's treachery."

R.A.N. OFFICERS RETURNING: Twenty-four Australian Naval officers who are returning to Australia after service in European waters were entertained at Australia House on Saturday.

DANCING BAN IN FINLAND: Dancing has been prohibited in Finland for duration of the war.

LABOR LEADERS MEET: The three Labor members of the UK War Cabinet — Mr. Attlee, Mr. Bevin and Mr. Morrison — conferred with the Labor Party's National Executive last week to clear up differences of opinion between Ministers and party officials on the advisability of a general election.

AUSTRALIAN PRISONERS DO COOLIE WORK IN BURMA

LEYTE, Sun.: Australian prisoners of war are being made to do coolie work in Burma. Magazines found on Leyte picture them performing humiliating tasks.

ONE photograph shows them cleaning the streets of Rangoon with crude native brooms and rakes.

The caption to the photo reads: "Burmese people line the sidewalk to look on with curiosity at the rare sight of British prisoners of war cleaning up the streets of Rangoon. Thanks to the Japanese forces, these Burmese people are now freed from the arrogant British."

The prisoners are shown wearing their Digger hats, short puttees, and shorts.

The magazines, printed in Japanese and English, were used for propaganda purposes throughout the Philippines.

The pictures show Allied troops in humiliating circumstances. One shows Lieut.-Gen. Wainwright's men marching through Manila to a prisoners' camp.

DOG SAVES FLYING BOMB VICTIMS

LONDON, Sun.: A black Alsatian mongrel, trained to detect people trapped alive, helped in the rescue of many people buried in debris when a flying bomb demolished a hotel on Friday. The dog growled as a signal to rescue squads.

SHIPBUILDING MAKES GOOD PROGRESS

CANBERRA, Sun.: By July last Australia had completed 63,900 tons of its 12,000 tons merchant shipbuilding programme, and two 9000-ton ships were nearing completion in Australian yards, the Supply and Shipping Department announced yesterday.

Considerable progress was now being made in the construction of merchant vessels of 9000, 4000 and 2000 tons, the Department added.

N.Z. VOLCANO ERUPTS

AUCKLAND, Sun.: Following a series of slight eruptions in the past month, the crater lake on Mount Ruapehu, in the North Island, erupted yesterday.

In a full-scale burst a column of steam and debris rose thousands of feet into the air. It was the biggest eruption since 1945, when a similar disturbance heaped debris two feet deep around the edges of the lake.

Before the actual eruption, several bursts of steam came from the crater, then a huge cloud of steam shot suddenly several thousand feet above the mountain. It hung there for 10 minutes and then blue mud and grit fell.

SERVICE SECTION

LOST: Spectacles in brown case. L. J. DAVIS, engineer, is advised that wrongly addressed parcel awaits him at this office.

PRINCE'S 'NANNY' AND COT FOR CANBERRA

LONDON, Sun.: The only furniture the Duke and Duchess of Gloucester intend to take to Australia is a cot for Prince Richard.

The Duchess is bringing a number of servants, including the children's "Nanny." She is a Miss Lightbody, and is described as a "sensible old-fashioned Scots woman," who has been with the Gloucesters since Prince William was born.

AUSTRALIA OBSERVES SOVIET ANNIVERSARY

MELBOURNE, Sun.: Russia's national day, the 27th anniversary of the foundation of the Soviet State, was celebrated here today with a procession and a public meeting at the West Melbourne Stadium.

The Commander-in-Chief of the Australian Military Forces (General Sir Thomas Blamey) today paid a tribute to the part played by Russian armies in the fight against Germany. He [illegible]

RAT POISON FOR GERMANS

LONDON, Sun.: An Ipswich vicar, Rev. H. C. Green, who sent a tin of rat poison to an appeal for comforts for German PsOW in Britain, has been censured by the Bishop of Ipswich.

THE Bishop said: "It was a poor joke and vulgar. Mr. Green is entitled to his own views, although they differ from mine regarding the appeal, but idle and ill-mannered jesting on such a serious matter is deplorable, especially in a clergyman.

"I can do nothing beyond telling him that his action is most reprehensible and has brought discredit to the Church."

Commenting on the Bishop's remarks, Mr. Green said: "I have received 201 letters, the majority of which support me. Many officers and men in the services, also clergymen of all denominations, have congratulated me."

The sponsor of the appeal admitted yesterday that he had [illegible]

Ace Pilot's 30 "Kills"

NEW YORK, Sun.: Commander David McCampbell, US Navy fighter pilot shot down nine planes and probably two more in one hour 35 minutes during the Philippines battle, bringing his total number of "kills" to 30.

Englishwoman Faces Death In Greece To Protect Australians

ATHENS, Sun.: Sentenced to death by the Gestapo for having refused to divulge the whereabouts of fugitive Australians, an Englishwoman bribed a guard and made an 11th hour escape, writes war correspondent Keith Hooper.

THE woman, Mrs. Kallinchos (formerly Evelyn Pawley, of Cardiff, Wales), will be remembered by Australians who escaped from Greece. Tall, slim, and red-haired, she was known to them as "Rose Marie" or "Ginger."

In peace days secretary to the president of an Athens power company, Evelyn joined the Greek "underground" immediately after the German occupation, and undertook the task of spiriting Allied servicemen from the country. She was arrested several times, brutally treated, and finally sentenced to death.

Evelyn, waiting in a cell to be shot, bribed a Bavarian guard with a gold ring. He permitted her to escape from the car in which she was being taken to Gestapo headquarters, after which she remained in hiding until the arrival of the British.

WHISKY TOO CHEAP FOR THIS G.I.

LONDON, Sun.: An American soldier entered a London hotel and asked for a bottle of whisky. When, incredibly, the publican produced one and asked for 25/9 (the regulation price), the soldier shook his head.

"I couldn't take the risk," he said. "I want the £4/10/ sort. The boys say you can't get a bottle under that."

The publican and others in the bar were unable to convince the soldier that nothing was wrong, and he left without buying.

WHALE UPSETS N.Z. FISHERMAN

WELLINGTON (NZ), Sat.: "With a flick of its 10ft. wide, barnacle-encrusted tail, a 70ft. whale yesterday lifted a launch almost out of water off Island Bay, near Perski, Akaroa Heads [illegible]

story was verified by two other fishermen who were nearby. A trawler owner, J. Gracia, reported that more whales were going north this season than ever before. He recently found himself [illegible]

ENTERTAINMENTS

AUSTRALIAN CIRCUIT — Tonight—Base HQ: "Arizona" (Jean Arthur, William Holden). Mainbang: Concert by "Tasmanians."

AMERICAN CIRCUIT — Tonight—No. 1: "Conflict" (Humphrey Bogart). No. 3: "Atlantic City" (Constance Moore, Jerry Colonna). No. 5: "Kansas City Kitty" (Joan Davis, Bob Crosby). No. 8: "Till We Meet Again" (Ray Milland, Barbara Britton). No. 10: "Bride By Mistake" [illegible]

NAZIS REEL BACK BEFORE NEW DRIVE IN HOLLAND

LONDON, Sun.: Blinded by smoke, scorched by flame-throwers and battered by artillery, remnants of the German 15th Army have been sent reeling back from strong defensive positions in SW Holland by a new British attack.

THE attack was launched by the British Second Army yesterday afternoon on a narrow front along the southern bank of the River Maas. By nightfall, it had driven the Germans back two miles, and brought the British forces to within four miles of the enemy's last escape route at Moerdijk.

Mass batteries of artillery softened up the German defences, entrenched behind a 30ft. wide canal, before the infantry went into the attack in assault boats behind a smoke screen.

Flame-throwers were used in large numbers against the enemy's defences. Chester Wilmot, BBC correspondent

SCORCHING ATTACK . . .

who watched the attack, reported that they had proved very successful. He saw Germans scorched by the blazing oil running dazedly out of what they had considered almost impregnable strongpoints.

The Germans now are gradually being herded into a small pockets between the British Second Army and Canadian and Polish troops to the west, who are closing in on the long broad estuary flowing into the Maas. Yesterday, these troops were reported only two miles from the estuary, and field dispatches reported that they were continuing to advance almost at will.

In the Scheldt Estuary, savage battles for control of the few remaining German batteries on Walcheren Island are continuing. British forces, fighting from house to house, are gradually reducing German pockets.

In Germany, heavily reinforced German tank and infantry formations have driven troops of the US First Army out of the town of Schmidt, 15 miles south-east of Aachen.

SLIGHT U.S. REVERSE . . .

Correspondents report, however, that waves of Thunderbolts have battered the town itself almost into rubble.

To the north, the lines of the First Army are holding firm against repeated enemy counter-blows, while, in eastern France, the US Third Army has launched a successful attack south of Metz. It was last reported making progress against strong resistance.

ROYAL NAVY UNITS SINK U-BOATS, WHIP LUFTWAFFE

LONDON, Sun.: British Home Fleet units, including aircraft carriers, scored a brilliant victory over German U-boats and planes during escort duties with an important Allied convoy to Russia and another back to Britain.

A British Admiralty statement to-day said that three U-boats were definitely sunk, with another three probably destroyed. Not one merchantman was damaged, but a naval sloop was lost when it was hit by a torpedo.

NIMITZ'S AIRMEN HIT AT AIRFIELDS & SHIPS

PEARL HARBOR, Sun.: US Army and Navy planes under the command of Admiral Chester W. Nimitz have bombed Japanese airfields and shipping in a two-days' operation against the Volcano and Bonin Islands groups.

A Pacific Fleet communique announced today that an enemy cargo ship was sunk, another left burning and two others were damaged in the actions.

NEW ROYAL NAVY PLANE

LONDON, Sun.: The Firefly, a two-seater fighter, is the latest aircraft of Britain's Fleet Air Arm.

It armament consists of four 20 mm. cannon in the wings, which fold for ship storage. The main wheels of the under-carriage fold inwards, and the tail-wheel also retracts. The Firefly's duties include reconnaissance and the occupant of the rear cockpit attends to navigational and radio duties on long flights.

Curtin In Hospital

MELBOURNE, Sun.: The Prime Minister (Mr. Curtin), who has been confined to bed here for several days, yesterday entered a private hospital on the recommendation of his doctors. They considered that he needed further rest before making the trip to Canberra. Mr. Curtin had hoped to be in Canberra tomorrow, but it is not expected that he will be able to travel for several days.

SOVIETS SNUB SWISS: PROTEST ON POLICY

LONDON, Sun.: The Soviet Government to-day formally announced its rejection of a request by Switzerland to re-establish diplomatic relations between the two countries. The Russian statement added that the Swiss Government had not revoked its pre-war foreign policy which was hostile to the interests of the USSR.

HEAVY DAMAGE BY U.S. B-29's TO RANGOON TARGETS

USAAF (India) HQ, Sun.: Pilots of reconnaissance aircraft which flew over Rangoon yesterday reported that fires were still smouldering from Friday's heavy attack by Super-Fortresses on the city's railway marshalling yards.

Pilots of the B-29's said the railway targets had been so severely damaged by the first wave of Super-Fortresses that following waves had difficulty in locating the yards.

They also reported that 22 Japanese fighters were airborne over the target areas, but made no attempts to ward off the attacks.

REICH CANAL BREACHED

LONDON, Sun.: US Liberators from Britain on Thursday breached the important Mittelland Canal at Minden (Germany)—one of the Reich's most important east-west inland waterways.

US Strategic Airforce headquarters announced today that bombs destroyed an 80ft. section of the canal and drained it dry for three miles. The canal links central and eastern Germany with the Ruhr and Rhineland.

KEYES FINDS FLAW IN HOME FRONT ATTITUDE

BRISBANE, Sun.: Admiral of the Fleet Lord Keyes, who watched the initial landing operations in the Philippines, disclosed yesterday that HMAS Australia which was damaged in action off Leyte, had been sent to an American Pacific base for repairs.

"At this base," he said, "they work 24 hours a day, as all soldiers and sailors must be prepared to do, compared with the home front in this country, where the number of hours to be worked a week are decided by some body of which I have no knowledge."

Japan Now Fifth-Rate Naval Power, Says Admiral

WASHINGTON, Sun.: As the result of its recent shattering defeats off Formosa and the Philippines, Japan had been reduced to a fifth-rate naval power, the commander of the US 58th Task Force (Vice-Adm. Mark A. Mitscher) said yesterday.

VICE-ADMIRAL MITSCHER is the first high-ranking American naval officer to return to the US since the Formosa and Philippines engagements, in which he said, Japan's aviation had suffered a very serious blow.

The US commander claimed that seven Japanese aircraft carriers—three more than announced officially by the Navy Department—were sunk in the Formosa and Philippines battles. Japan now had only a few battleships, a couple of major carriers and several small carriers, he said.

The battle off Formosa was the greatest naval-air engagement of the entire war, he added. The Japanese put everything they had into their counter-attacks, but American fliers held an eight to one advantage in combat.

Between January 29 and October 27, the 58th Task Force—said to be the greatest striking power of its kind in the world—destroyed or put out of action 4425 enemy aircraft, and sunk or damaged 292 Japanese warships and 388 merchant ships. Total of Japanese tonnage sunk in this period was 1,125,000.

GREECE LIBERATED: NAZIS FACE TRAP IN YUGOSLAVIA

ATHENS, Sun.: After three years of German occupation, Greece has now been completely liberated. Allied headquarters announced to-day that the last Nazi rearguard crossed into Yugoslavia on Friday night.

EARLIER reports from BBC correspondent Douglas Willis said pilots of Greek-based RAF planes reported on their return to base yesterday that they could find no signs of any Germans in the whole of Greece. The liberation of the 50,000 square miles of Greek territory was accomplished in less than a month.

Willis said that bad weather had prevented British planes from operating against the fleeing enemy forces over the last few miles of territory between Greece and the Yugoslav frontier. The Nazis carried out extensive "scorched earth" operations in their flight, and blew up roads and railway lines and bridges.

Fierce battles were in progress yesterday inside Yugoslavia, where Marshal Tito's partisans were engaged in operations against German forces retreating from Greece. There was heavy fighting for Monastir, hub of enemy communications in Western Yugoslav, and farther east for the key town of Skoplje.

RETREATING ENEMY MASSACRED GREEKS

ATHENS, Sun.: **"Anyone who has the slightest leaning towards Germany should be made to drive through the villages I have seen in my trip by car from Athens to the Yugoslav border."**

This statement was made by BBC correspondent John Nixon in a dispatch to London to-day. At one village, said Nixon, he was met by 25 ragged children and three women with tears in their eyes, who told him that the Nazis had massacred the entire male population of the village and had burned down every building there.

Flying Bombs Fall Again On Southern England

LONDON, Sun.: At least five persons died last night when Nazi flying bombs struck southern England, where the first daylight attack for two months was also experienced yesterday. One of the German "pick-a-back" planes which launched the bombs during the night was shot down. Several of the robots also fell to RAF fighters and AA defences.

SIR JOHN DILL DEAD

WASHINGTON, Sun.: Field-Marshal Sir John Dill, chief of the British Military Mission to the United States, died here last night at a private hospital after an illness lasting several months. He was 63 years old.

Sir John, who entered the British Army in 1901, saw service in South Africa and France, and was Chief of the Imperial General Staff before his appointment to Washington in 1942.

HEAVY CASUALTIES ON BOTH SIDES IN ITALY

ROME, Sun.: **Allied casualties in Italy during the past six months totalled 116,150, compared with German casualties estimated at 194,000, Gen. Sir Harold Alexander's HQ reported to-day.**

With rains and thunderstorms continuing on the land fronts, activity is being confined largely to patrolling. Supplies to the Eighth Army now have to be taken across flooded rivers on ferries and hastily improvised bridges.

HOW TYPHOONS HELPED LIBERATE FLUSHING

LONDON, Sun.: **Rocket-firing Typhoons aided in the final stages of the liberation of the major part of Flushing, when they blasted and set on fire a luxury hotel in which hundreds of Germans were holding out.**

This was disclosed to-day by a spokesman of the RAF Second Tactical Force, who said that the Typhoons were sent out in response to an urgent signal from the commander of the Allied ground forces. Their appearance was timed to precede a bayonet assault by British infantry, but, before the assault could get under way, the Germans were streaming out of the hotel to surrender.

Little Time Lost Through Strikes In Britain

CANBERRA, Sun.: Time lost through industrial disputes in England during the war has averaged only 55 minutes a year for each worker, according to figures released yesterday by the British High Commissioner's office here. "The loss represents .003 per cent of the total hours worked," the statement declared. "This is an infinitesimal price to be paid for maintaining in wartime the democratic principle of the workers' right to collective action."

Late Flashes From World's Newsrooms

● ***INSURANCE:*** The payment of war damage insurance premiums by Australian property owners will be allowed to lapse from the end of this month, according to an official announcement in Canberra.

● ***RETURNED:*** Professor Burstall, of the Chair of Engineering at Sydney University, returned to Australia from England on Saturday. He had been engaged in work connected with the production of secret war weapons for the British War Office.

● ***HOME:*** The former Governor-General of Australia (Lord Gowrie), accompanied by Lady Gowrie, arrived in London on Saturday. They were greeted at Euston Station by representatives of the British Government.

● ***BEAUFORTS:*** The director of the Beaufort Division of the Department of Aircraft Production (Mr. John Storey), on his return to-day from operational areas in New Guinea and N.W. Australia, said he was satisfied R.A.A.F. pilots had gained confidence in Australian-built aircraft. Beauforts were in every way suitable for operations in tropical conditions, he added.

● ***UNITY:*** Talks between the Prime Minister of the Royal Yugoslav Government (Dr. Subasitch) and members of Marshal Tito's Partisan Government are reported to be progressing well. A communique from Marshal Tito's headquarters yesterday said it was hoped that a unified Cabinet would be formed soon.

● ***FUNERAL:*** The King and Queen, European Royalties, peers and ambassadors attended the funeral of Princess Beatrice, great aunt of the King, at St. George's Chapel, Windsor. Princess Beatrice was the last surviving child of Queen Victoria.

● ***SYMPATHY:*** The Acting Governor-General of Australia (Sir Winston Dugan) has received a message from the Duke of Gloucester expressing regret at the loss of life on HMAS Australia, when the cruiser was hit by a Japanese bomber off Leyte.

● ***EDEN:*** The British Foreign Secretary (Mr. Eden) returned to London yesterday from Moscow, Cairo and Italy, where he had held discussions with the C-in-C (Gen. Sir Harold Alexander).

STOP PRESS

PHILIPPINES: American troops on the west coast of Leyte Island have opened a new offensive to "squeeze" out Japanese forces concentrated at their remaining base of Ormoc. Preliminary reports from General MacArthur's HQ says fierce fight-

GREECE: Allied HQ in Athens has announced that British reinforcements have been landed at the recently liberated port of Salonika, in north-eastern Greece. Correspondents suggest that the Allied command is building up forces for a move into Yugoslavia.

T H E

R E E F E R

G A Z E T T E

* *

627th QM Refrig. Co. (F)   Saturday, December 30, 1944   Vol. I, No. 9

* *

EDITORIAL

Got some bad news for the column, today. This place is really going 'garrison'!!! Bend your ear to this soldier's lament.

Effective 1 Jan/45, every organization on the base will be inspected by representatives from Headquarters, at least once a month. These inspections will be conducted along the same lines as those Saturday morning affairs back in the States. Every man will be present in formation, in prescribed uniform and with fresh haircuts. Add a full field display on bunks and a thorough check of the area to that and it'll take you back a year or more. Also, you will be called upon to refamiliarize yourselves with various military subjects. Lectures on each topic selected, will be held for 2 hours every month.

Then of course, you are already aware of the fact you will fall out every morning by platoons in company formation for roll call and policing. (This in lieu of road marches).

In a 'combat outfit', this, of course, is necessary, but how about a service unit that's doing its job and doing it well?

It's not the place of a mere 1st Sgt. to question the sagacity of the learned gentlemen who dictate the policies, but I'm like you, sometimes I wonder what the reason is, for some of the things we do. However, they probably know a hell of a lot more than I, or they wouldn't be on top. Also disagreement disrupts unity and we've got too much at stake [illegible]

So, although, I may be a sad soldier, I'm also going to be a good one and do what I'm told willingly and without question.

* * * * * * * * * * * * * * * *

STAFF

* * * * * * * * * * * * * * * *

1st Sgt. Francis - Editor
Cpl. Koch - Associate Ed.

ROUND AND ABOUT

We're having a 'rock-picking bee' tonight, at 1715. Everybody is invited. In fact, BE THERE!!!!!

Seeing some of those old boys like Eubanks, Wagoner and Ganobcik cavort out on the basketball court, makes one believe there is something in that old adage 'Life begins at 40'.

Papa Bears & Johnnie Robertson pulled out yesterday for parts unknown. Good luck, fellas. I hope we'll be seeing you.

Carroll is losing his verbal sparring partner, Eldridge. I wonder who he'll be feuding with next?

Looks like Lemmons & Gardner may be boarded one of these days. Better get down to the 4th General and see them.

If Van and Milt were in a match race and hit the finish tape at the same time, it would be interesting to see the 'photo-finish', wouldn't it?

If I didn't know better, I'd say that Ming Dong came from Brooklyn. He makes more noise at the ball games than a 'Long Tom'.

There's a certain wearer of gold bars in this outfit, that's getting awfully careless about where he parts his garbage. A word to the wise, Lt. That bed belongs to the editor of a 'scandal sheet'.

* * * * * * * * * * * * *

ADS & NOTICES

Basketball game tonite!!

Reefers vs 93 Recon. The truck will be leaving at 1800 from the top of the hill.
This is the last game of League games and promised to be a good one.

SPORT-LIGHT

In a Wildcat League basket ball game played before a crowd of 52(000) Thursday night, the Gators came to life and chewed the hapless Grizzlies into submission, 22 - 16.

Both teams playing much improved ball, gave a good exhibition. The score was close until the final quarter, when the winners put on a spurt that gave them a substantial margin which they never relinquished.

The amazing Gators, showing the result of nightly practices, fielded a first class ball club. Their passing was swift and accurate, working the ball under the basket for frequent 'shorts'. The attack was well balanced and featured teamwork which permitted no individual stars. Kefalas played a fine floor game with Yates collecting 8 points for top scoring honors. Incidentally, something new has been added to the game. Shields has perfected a kind of "horizontal plummet" shot which travels on a level plane just skimming the basket ring, then stops dead and drops thru the hoop. Sure saves a lot of time.

Individually, the Grizzlies all play good ball but they don't do it together. Suggest, Captain Copeland, that you take that galaxy of stars on the court a couple of times before your next game and mould them into a unit.

In the second game, the All-Stars almost sent some ice cubes to hell, when they sur- [illegible] with a shifth offence and a defense that was tighter than a bull's --s in fly time. The Reefers, although winning 21-17, made a tough job out of it. Maybe it's because they were 'off form' and then maybe the opposition was better. Next game will tell!!

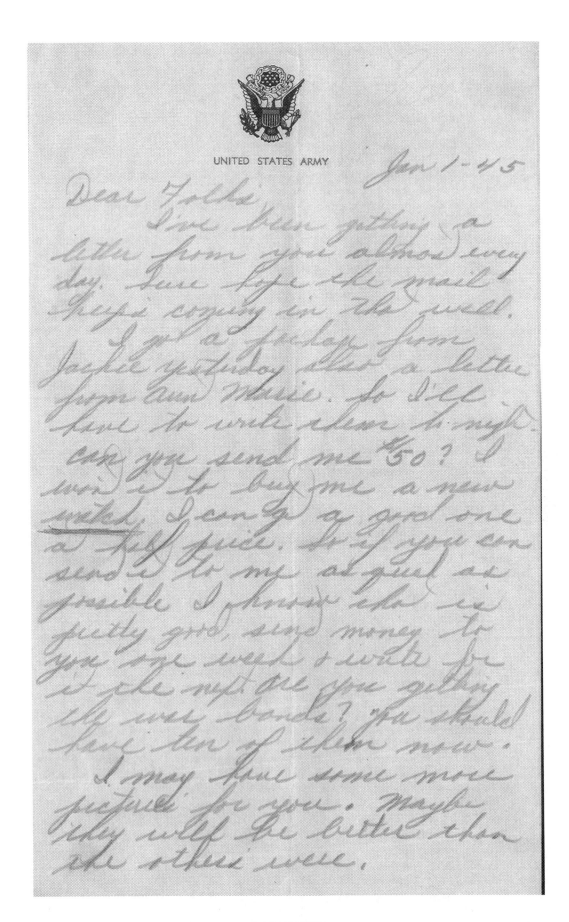

UNITED STATES ARMY

Jan 1-45

Dear Folks

I've been getting a letter from you almost every day. Sure hope the mail keeps coming in that well.

I got a package from Jackie yesterday also a letter from Aunt Marie. So I'll have to write them to-night.

Can you send me $50? I want it to buy me a new watch. I can get a good one at half price. So if you can send it to me as quick as possible I know that is pretty good, send money to you one week & write for it the next. Are you getting the war bonds? You should have ten of them now.

I may have some more pictures for you. Maybe they will be better than the others were.

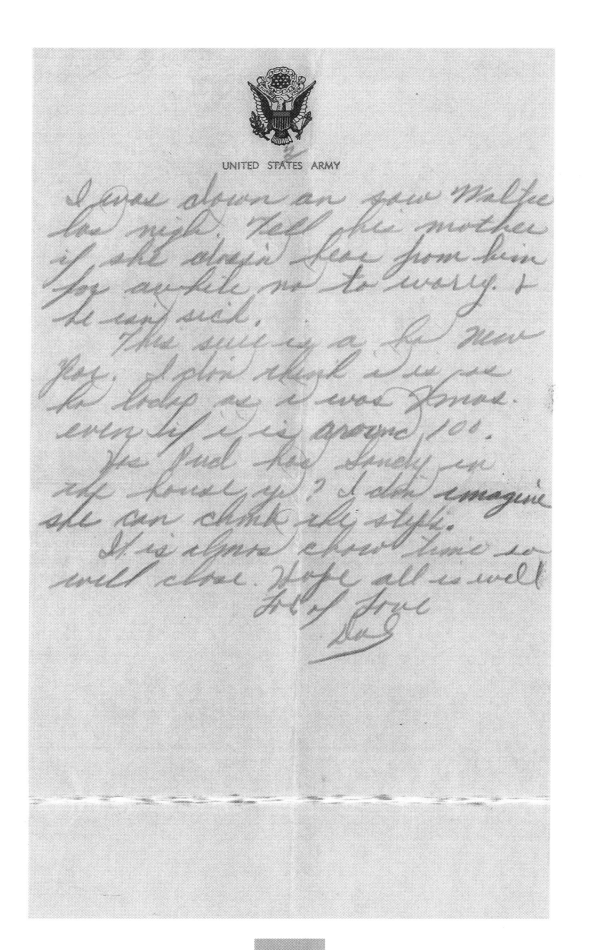

UNITED STATES ARMY

I was down an saw Walfe
last night. Tell his mother
if she doesn't hear from him
for awhile not to worry. &
he ain't sick.

This sure is a far [illegible] New
Year. I don't think it is as
hot today as it was Xmas.
even tho it is around 100.

Ive bet Ma's lonely in
the house, eh? I don't imagine
she can climb the steps.

It is almost chow time so
will close. Hope all is well

Lot of Love

Bud

Jan 21-45

Dear Folks,

I had one letter from you today, it was the first one I've gotten all week. Got three letters from Mickie yesterday, so I'll have to write her when I finish this to you.

I spent most the morning swimming, the water sure was nice, an clear for once. you could see 20 ft. deep. I think there is a lot of pretty color here. Dad should be here to go swimming with me. I expect he would rather make snow balls. I know I would.

We really had some good ice cream last night. There was six of us an we ate two gallon. so I guess we sure had enough for once. We are going to make some more tomorrow night. I think I could be a first class bachelor when I get out of here. Mickie told me she was learning to cook, so I wasn't worrying about going hungry. The main thing she said was that she had the money for any kind of a house

3

I would like to live in. What you think of that? Don't tell me that would be like taking candy from a baby. Think I can go along in that for as well. But that would be a good deal.

I sent you the yanks today so you should get them by March. I don't have a thing to send you for your birthday. Maybe I can find you a V-mail birthday card. How is Dad an Sandy doing? Has she fell on the ice? Or does he ride her when its slick? Has Dad killed any more ducks? Or has he run out of shells? He should be here we would go a wild hog hunting.

Have you ever bought the car? Or can you find one? You can forget about the 50 dollars for, if you have seen it when I get it I'll send it back for I can't get a watch.

I can't think of any thing else to write so will close. Hope all is well.

Lots of Love

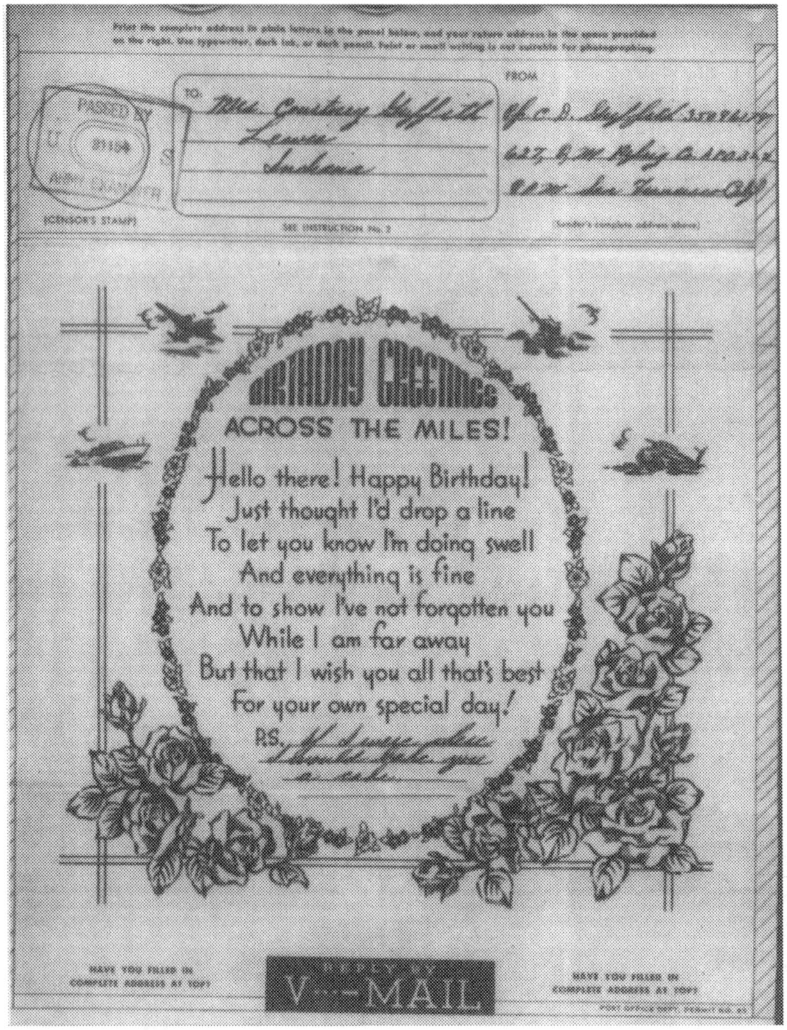
TO:
FROM
PASSED BY
(CENSOR'S STAMP)
SEE INSTRUCTION No. 2
BIRTHDAY GREETINGS
ACROSS THE MILES!
Hello there! Happy Birthday!
Just thought I'd drop a line
To let you know I'm doing swell
And everything is fine
And to show I've not forgotten you
While I am far away
But that I wish you all that's best
For your own special day!
P.S.
HAVE YOU FILLED IN COMPLETE ADDRESS AT TOP?
REPLY BY
V---MAIL
HAVE YOU FILLED IN COMPLETE ADDRESS AT TOP?

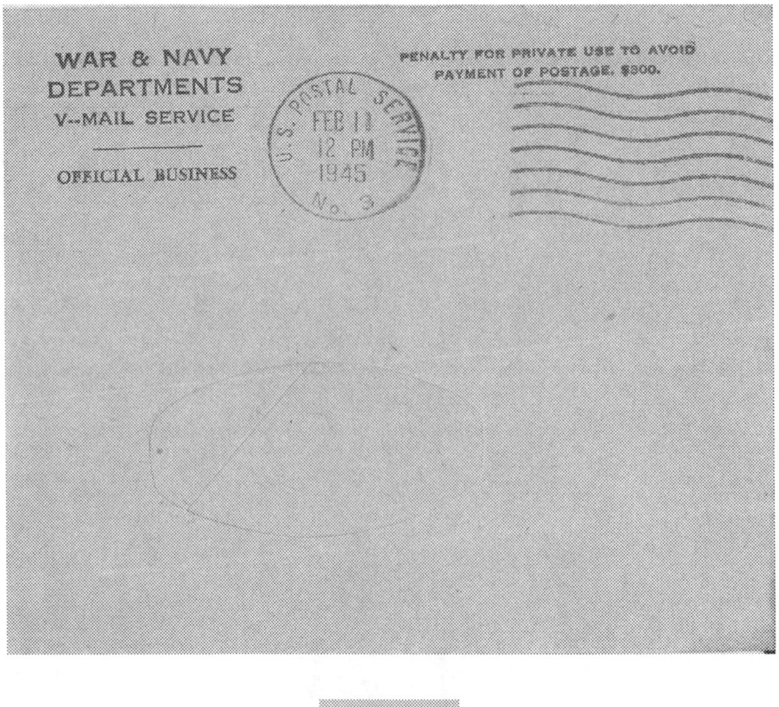
WAR & NAVY
DEPARTMENTS
V--MAIL SERVICE
OFFICIAL BUSINESS
U.S. POSTAL SERVICE
FEB 11
12 PM
1945
No. 3
PENALTY FOR PRIVATE USE TO AVOID
PAYMENT OF POSTAGE, $300.

March 23

Dear Folks,

I received six letters from you today they were the first I've had for almost two weeks. Hope you are getting my letters better than that. Sure hated to hear about Junior, if he is only reported missing maybe they will find him.

Was Buzz drafted? I bet she sure hated to go. Dad sure will have a lot of work to do this spring with him gone. Maybe the war will be over by this fall an we can help him pick the corn. If you need any money don't be afraid to cash those bonds.

I've written Angeline about six letters since they have wrote me, so you can tell them I'm waiting until they write. Maybe that will make her feel better. Was father or brother? What's been wrong with her? You never did say.

I haven't ever got the package you sent maybe it will be here soon.

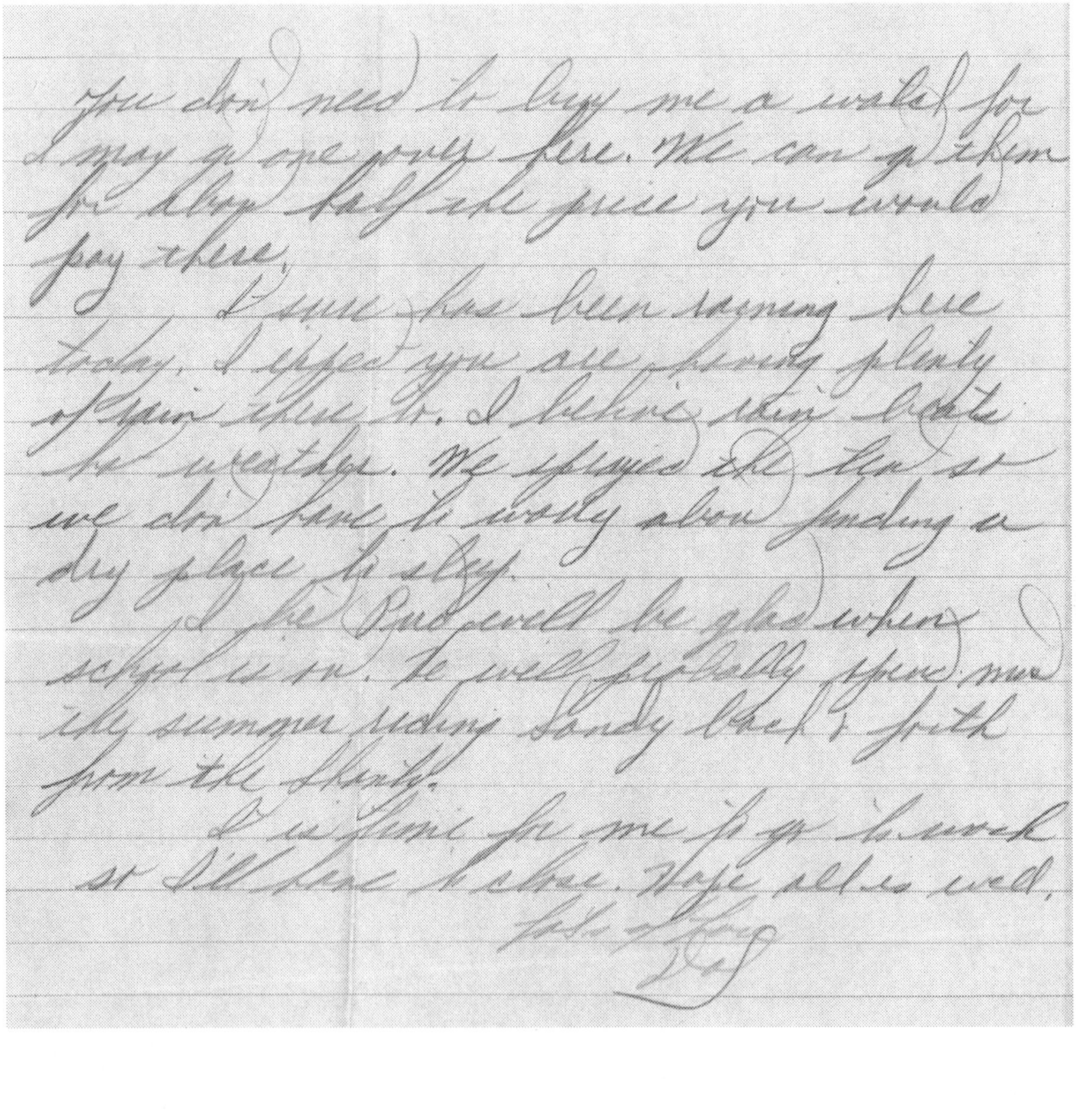
You don't need to buy me a watch for I may get one over here. We can get them for about half the price you would pay there.

It sure has been raining here today. I expect you are having plenty of rain there too. I believe [illegible] [illegible] the weather. We sprayed the tent so we don't have to worry about finding a dry place to sleep.

I bet Bud will be glad when school is on. He will probably sure miss this summer riding Sandy back & forth from the shanty.

It is time for me to go to work so I'll have to close. Hope all is well.

Lots of Love
Dad

June 16

Dear Folks,

I know you have been worrying since you haven't heard from me for so long but as you probably know we had another trip since.

We are now up North right on the tip of Luzon. You can't imagine how it looks; all of the buildings, homes etc have been destroyed. The people are awful nice but in need of food & clothing. We came here on an LST & had to sleep on deck but the water was nice and calm so we had a nice trip. [illegible] sea sick. ha.

I went to a dance last

night. I really had a swell time. Some of the girls are beautiful. They are only about five feet tall and have black hair and brown eyes. They always ride away as people go back home.

So I think I'm going to like this place a lot better than Mrs. S. A. The only thing bad about it, prices are sky high.

I sent you three dollars to get a movie one dollar for a soft drink, so you can figure why I stopped the ten for.

I got 24 letters yesterday so it looks like I'm really going to stay busy for the next week or so

3

How much did you get
for Nellie? Did Jesse ever
get any good out of her. I
guess she would of been
better off if you hadn't
bought her. Did you get
all of the corn picked? Sure
hope so. I'm going to get
me a garden out here. If
I can find any seeds
you can buy almost any
kind of fruits from the
people here. But the way it's
looking it's getting a little harder
to get.

It's chow time so I'd
better close. Will write more
tomorrow night. Hope all
are well.

With Love

Earl

June 17

Dear Folks,

I hope you have received one of my letters telling you I'm O.K. How long did it take for it to reach you?

I think the mail will travel faster from here than it did from N.G. I sure hope it does any way.

Sure was glad to hear Dad has all the corn planted. You even had me worried.

The soil here is the same as we have in the bottom sandy as heck. I bet it would raise some corn.

We have a pretty nice area to live in, plenty of green grass alongside a cement highway, so it beats New G.

all to heck.

I meant to go to the show to-night but it rained me out. I have plenty of letter's to write, so that's what I'm going to do for the next four hrs. ha.

Could you send me $25. we haven't been paid for two mos. so I'm almost broke. I will send it back to you as soon as we get paid.

Has Rube heard from Dale? Tell her not to worry, for these times they don't see land for two or three mos. so they don't have a chance to send out mail. By the way I have the same out fit he has. You look like a scare crow. ha.

3

I wrote Frankie a letter last night. Had five from here yesterday so thought it was about time I was writing her.

I saw an old 34 Ford today it really made me homesick. How does the old Ford run? Can Pa drive it? We'll have to get us a new one when I get home. If I get writing for more money I won't be able to go [illegible] unless I send a little first.

I can go to school for four years with all expense paid also $75 a month on top of it. I think that's what I'd better do, don't you?

Will better close and write some more

Lots of Love Dad

June 29

Dear Folks,

I wrote Fayetta a letter this morning so thought I'd better write you a father a letter this after-noon, for if I wait until to-night I'll probably end up going to the show without writing.

It's turned off a little cooler today sure hope it stays that way sometime. I think it gets hotter here than it did in F.G.

Has Dad ever got the corn plowed? Sure hope it dryes off long enough for him to get all the soy beans planted. He will have to raise rice if it keeps raining so. I was out in the country yesterday saw a lot of rice

2

fields, but very few corn fields. I guess rice is their main crop. An do they ever like to eat it. They fill a tub or box with it then they all set down around it an start eating, no silverware of any kind. I guess the old saying "you're where made before forks" still holds true over here.

Does Dad still hook Sandy to the sled, or is he afraid she will run off with him again? Aunt Marie wrote an told me about her teaching Pud S.; life must be some fun too.

I hear they are going to change the point system, if they do I'll have ten more points, sure hope they do maybe I'll get home sooner. The way it is now I'll never get home until after the war is over.

They just now had mail call. I didn't get any from you but I got three from Mother. Sometimes I think that's all she does write letters. I've got as high as six from her in one day. I do almost that good. I write her once every two weeks. I think I'll stop writing that often. She has too many bright ideas. Ha.

We took some pictures yesterday, as soon as I get them developed I'll send them to you. Have you ever found any films? I imagine they are still hard to get. Well I'd better close, an take a shower.

Lots of love [Dad]

Sept. 15-45

Dear Folks,

I got four letters from you today, they were the first I've gotten since we left Manila. We are now about 90 miles south of Manila at a staging area. It doesn't look like we are going to stay here long for we loaded all of equipment on the boat this morning so I imagine we will leave here tonight or early in the morning. We are going on a L.S.T. so we should have a nice trip. It only takes eight days to go to Japan from here, so we should be there by next Sunday.

2

Hope we don't have to stay
there long, for I've got all
this army I want, ha.

You kept asking if I ever
got the 25.°° Well yes I got that
about two mos. ago.

How does Bud like school
this year? Aunt Mase wrote
an told me about him seeing
a cow-boy show. He will be
so big I won't know him
when I get home.

Aunt Mase said she hadn't
heard from me for months -
you surely don't get all my letters
for I've been writing almost every
day. I know this is very
short, but we are going to get
ready to move. Think all of us will
Write when we land

Lots of Love

Dad

Sept. 31-45

Dear Folks,

Well, we have landed safe an sound, we docked at Yokohama an came on up to Tokyo by truck. We are almost in the center of town. Really have a nice building to live in. It use to be a school for Japanese army officers, It is a three story building, with hot & cold water showers ect. so I guess one couldn't ask for better.

That old saying one fire bomb, would burn Tokyo up is a lot of B.S. for they have the same buildings here as we have there. That is whats left of them. ha. I dont think it is torn up as bad as Manila

side, anyway what I've seen
of it hasn't been hurt much.
Coming up here last night
one of the trucks had a
flat tire, a Jap man came an
helped him change it, also
brought a pan of water &
a towel for the driver to
wash with after he fixed the
tire. But I still don't trust them
an neither does anyone else.
We really had some bad
ride coming up here. an did
I ever get sea sick. we ran
into a storm an was it
ever a bad one. The water
came up over the deck several
times, No one got hurt, but
a lot of them lost their
equipment.

3

They recounted the points
an I have 58 now. it
may be I'll get by the first
of the year. They are discharg-
ing all men with 90 points
now. an the first of Nov.
the are going to lower it
to 80, sure wish I had two
more points for if I did I
might be home by Xmas.

We got another battle star
for the Philippines, that
makes us two now. We
also have five ribbons.
I know we sure earned them.

Well it is getting late an I'm
really tired so will close. Hope
all is well.

Lots of Love
Dad

Print the complete address in plain letters in the panel below, and your return address in the space provided on the right. Use typewriter, dark ink, or dark pencil. Faint or small writing is not suitable for photographing.

(CENSOR'S STAMP)

TO: Mr. Mrs. C. L. [illegible]
Lewis
Indiana

SEE INSTRUCTION NO. 2

FROM 35196179
Pfc. C. D. [illegible]
427 Q.M. [illegible] Co. APO 503
c/o P.M. San Francisco Calif
Oct. 5-45

(Sender's complete address above)

Dear Folks

I had three letters from you today, they were the first I've gotten since we've been here. We can't get any air mail stamps here, so if you don't get any thing but V-mail letters send me some stamps ha.

You keep asking if I ever got the money order. Sure I got that two mos. ago. That's what I bought that picture & pocket book with. Have you ever got it? We took over a big ice plant here. Sure have got it easy. The Japs do all the work. About all we do is stand around an see that they do it. If they don't work they sure wish they had of. One of them brought me a big painting. I'll send it to you when I get something to wrap it in. Boy is it ever cold here. We almost freeze to death after being in New Guinea. That's one place I never want to see again ha. Well I should be home in Feb. If I had two more points which would make me sixty, I would be there by Xmas. I want Dad to cash two of those $50 bonds an buy a new 20 gauge automatic, for I want one an he can use it to quail hunt with this winter. So let's buy it Dad ha. Well must close. Hope all is well. Lots of love Bob

HAVE YOU FILLED IN COMPLETE ADDRESS AT TOP?

V-MAIL

HAVE YOU FILLED IN COMPLETE ADDRESS AT TOP?

U. S. GOVERNMENT PRINTING OFFICE : 1943 16—[illegible]

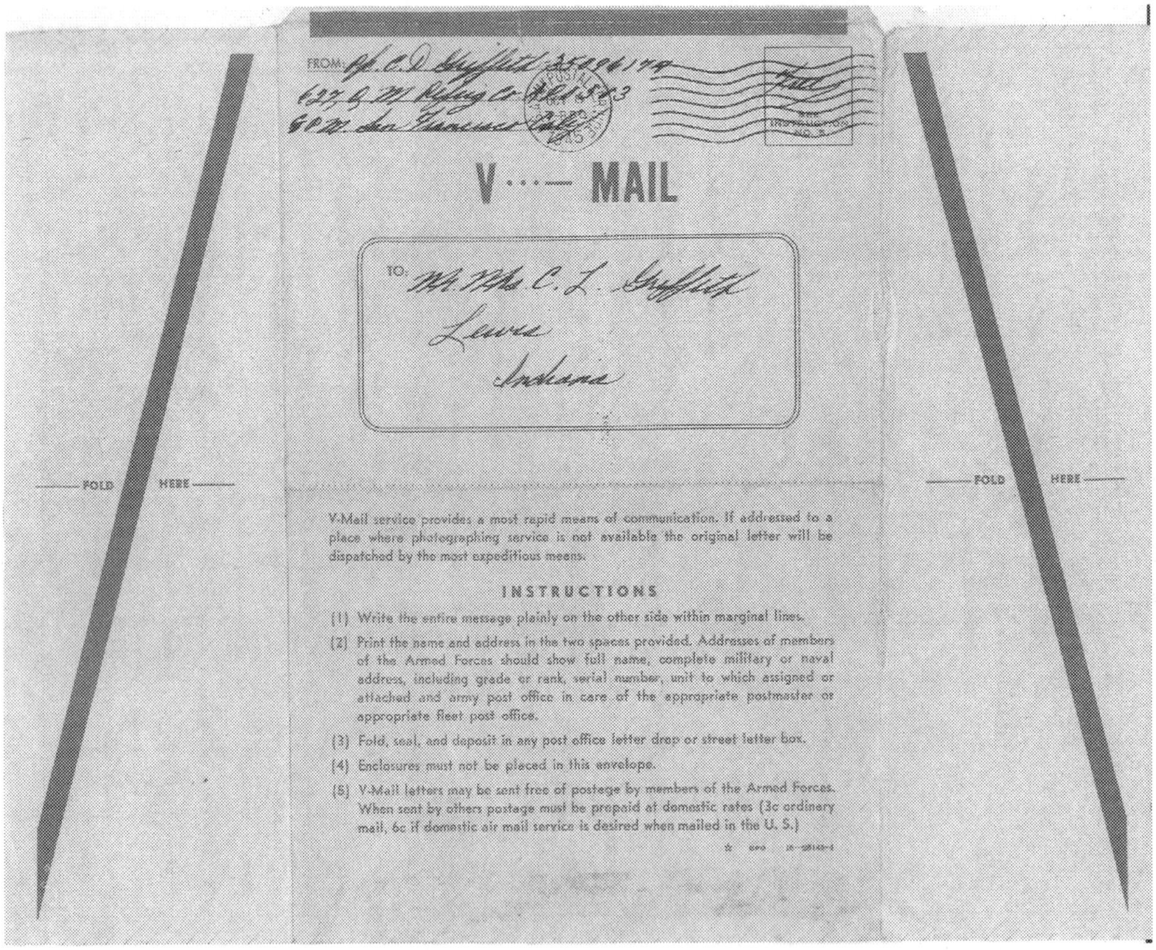
FROM:

V···— MAIL

TO:

Lewis

Indiana

FOLD HERE

V-Mail service provides a most rapid means of communication. If addressed to a place where photographing service is not available the original letter will be dispatched by the most expeditious means.

INSTRUCTIONS

(1) Write the entire message plainly on the other side within marginal lines.

(2) Print the name and address in the two spaces provided. Addresses of members of the Armed Forces should show full name, complete military or naval address, including grade or rank, serial number, unit to which assigned or attached and army post office in care of the appropriate postmaster or appropriate fleet post office.

(3) Fold, seal, and deposit in any post office letter drop or street letter box.

(4) Enclosures must not be placed in this envelope.

(5) V-Mail letters may be sent free of postage by members of the Armed Forces. When sent by others postage must be prepaid at domestic rates (3c ordinary mail, 6c if domestic air mail service is desired when mailed in the U. S.)

FOLD HERE

Oct. 30-45

Dear Folks,

I didn't hear from you again today. Hope every one is O.K. I just finished a letter to Janice & one to Aunt Marie, so you see I've really been on the beam writing letters to-night.

I meant to go to the show but it's to darn cold to get out side. Guess I've changed since I was home. ha.

We didn't do much today went to work at nine & came back at eleven, I spent the whole afternoon in bed.

I got two packages from you yesterday. Everything came thru just fine. I really needed those cigarettes & pipe. We haven't been

issued any for almost a month.
We have been opening C. rat.
just for the cigarettes. The
Japs sure will pay for cigarettes
they give you a yen apiece, which
amount to about eight cents.

Has Dad ever got the new
shot gun? How is the corn
picking coming along? Is he
going to get it all in before
the 10th.? Did he ever get
Browns pond built?

What's the matter with
Jackie? I haven't heard from
her since I was in New
G. Hope they are all well.

I know this isn't much of
a letter but I really haven't
any thing to write about. Guess
a page or two is better than
none at all. Lots of Love

DL

Nov. 22 - 45

Dear Folks,

Well two years ago today I was home. it sure seems more than two years to me, more like ten. ha.

I haven't heard from you for almost two weeks, hope everyone is well.

We really had a swell Thanksgiving dinner, Turkey dressing mashed Potatoes Celery fresh cabbage peas gravy pie & ice cream. I bet that is a better meal than most people had back there,

We really got some good news today the first of Dec. we are relieved from duty, that means we will be on our way home some time after the first. Sure would like to be there for Xmas, but I imagine we will spend Xmas on the boat. Maybe I'll be there for new years.

Tell Dad not to kill all of the quails for I am going to violate the law a little when I get there, ha. an I bet he does to.

Nov. 22 - 45

Dear Folks,

Well two years ago today I was home. it sure seems more than two years tho' me, more like ten. ha.

I haven't heard from you for almost two weeks, hope everyone is well.

We really had a swell Thanksgiving dinner, Turkey dressing mashed Potatoes Celery fresh cabbage peas gravy pie & ice cream. I bet that is a better meal than most people had back there.

We really got some good news today, the first of Dec. we are relieved from duty, that means we will be on our way home some time after the first. Sure would like to be there for Xmas, but I imagine we will spend Xmas on the boat. Maybe I'll be there for new years.

Tell Dad not to kill all of the quails for I'm going to violate the law a little when I get there. ha. an I bet he does to.

38006

ENLISTED RECORD AND REPORT OF SEPARATION

HONORABLE DISCHARGE

INDIANA BONUS APPLIED FOR

25 2 13 BLR

1. LAST NAME - FIRST NAME - MIDDLE INITIAL	2. ARMY SERIAL NO.	3. GRADE	4. ARM OR SERVICE	5. COMPONENT
GRIFFITH COURTNEY D	35 096 179	TEC-5	QMC	AUS

6. ORGANIZATION	7. DATE OF SEPARATION	8. PLACE OF SEPARATION
627TH QM REFRIGERATION CO	25 JAN 46	SEP CEN CAMP ATTERBURY IND

9. PERMANENT ADDRESS FOR MAILING PURPOSES	10. DATE OF BIRTH	11. PLACE OF BIRTH
GEN DEL LEWIS CLAY IND	18 APR 1924	LEWIS IND

12. ADDRESS FROM WHICH EMPLOYMENT WILL BE SOUGHT	13. COLOR EYES	14. COLOR HAIR	15. HEIGHT	16. WEIGHT	17. NO. DEPEND.
SEE #9	BLUE	BROWN	5'9"	169 LBS.	0

18. RACE: WHITE	NEGRO	OTHER (specify)	19. MARITAL STATUS: SINGLE	MARRIED	OTHER (specify)	20. U.S. CITIZEN: YES	NO	21. CIVILIAN OCCUPATION AND NO.
X			X			X		STUDENT HIGH SCHOOL X-02

MILITARY HISTORY

22. DATE OF INDUCTION	23. DATE OF ENLISTMENT	24. DATE OF ENTRY INTO ACTIVE SERVICE	25. PLACE OF ENTRY INTO SERVICE
2 MAR 43		9 MAR 43	FORT BENJAMIN HARRISON IND

SELECTIVE SERVICE DATA	26. REGISTERED: YES	NO	27. LOCAL S.S. BOARD NO.	28. COUNTY AND STATE	29. HOME ADDRESS AT TIME OF ENTRY INTO SERVICE
	X		1	CLAY CO IND	SEE #9

30. MILITARY OCCUPATIONAL SPECIALTY AND NO.	31. MILITARY QUALIFICATION AND DATE (i.e., infantry, aviation and marksmanship badges, etc.)
SUPPLY CLERK 835	RIFLE MARKSMAN

32. BATTLES AND CAMPAIGNS
NEW GUINEA SOUTHERN PHILIPPINES

33. DECORATIONS AND CITATIONS ASIATIC-PACIFIC THEATER RIBBON W/2 BRONZE STAR; AMERICAN THEATER RIBBON; GOOD CONDUCT RIBBON; WORLD WAR II VICTORY MEDAL PHILIPPINE LIBERATION RIBBON

34. WOUNDS RECEIVED IN ACTION
NONE

35. LATEST IMMUNIZATION DATES: SMALLPOX	TYPHOID	TETANUS	OTHER (specify)	36. SERVICE OUTSIDE CONTINENTAL U.S. AND RETURN: DATE OF DEPARTURE	DESTINATION	DATE OF ARRIVAL
~~JAN 44~~	~~JAN 45~~	~~JAN 44~~	~~FLU OCT 45~~	1 MAR 44	ASIATIC-PAC	5 APR 44
				NOT AVAILABLE	USA	16 JAN 46

37. TOTAL LENGTH OF SERVICE: CONTINENTAL SERVICE YEARS	MONTHS	DAYS	FOREIGN SERVICE YEARS	MONTHS	DAYS	38. HIGHEST GRADE HELD
1	0	1	1	10	16	TEC-5

39. PRIOR SERVICE
NONE

40. REASON AND AUTHORITY FOR SEPARATION
CONVN OF GOVT AR 615-365 RR 1-1 DEMOBILIZATION 15 DEC 44

41. SERVICE SCHOOLS ATTENDED	42. EDUCATION (Years): GRAMMAR	HIGH SCHOOL	COLLEGE
NONE	8	4	0

PAY DATA VOU 25193

43. LONGEVITY FOR PAY PURPOSES: YEARS	MONTHS	DAYS	44. MUSTERING OUT PAY: TOTAL	THIS PAYMENT	45. SOLDIER DEPOSITS	46. TRAVEL PAY	47. TOTAL AMOUNT, NAME OF DISBURSING OFFICER
2	10	24	$ 300	$ 100	0	$ 4.55	232 79 BB CALLAWAY LT COL F

INSURANCE NOTICE

IMPORTANT IF PREMIUM IS NOT PAID WHEN DUE OR WITHIN THIRTY-ONE DAYS THEREAFTER, INSURANCE WILL LAPSE. MAKE CHECKS OR MONEY ORDERS PAYABLE TO THE TREASURER OF THE U. S. AND FORWARD TO COLLECTIONS SUBDIVISION, VETERANS ADMINISTRATION, WASHINGTON 25, D. C.

48. KIND OF INSURANCE: Nat. Serv.	U.S. Govt.	None	49. HOW PAID: Allotment	Direct to V.A.	50. Effective Date of Allotment Discontinuance	51. Date of Next Premium Due (One month after 50)	52. PREMIUM DUE EACH MONTH	53. INTENTION OF VETERAN TO: Continue	Continue Only	Discontinue
X			X		JAN 46	28 FEB 46	$ 6.50			X

54. RIGHT THUMB PRINT

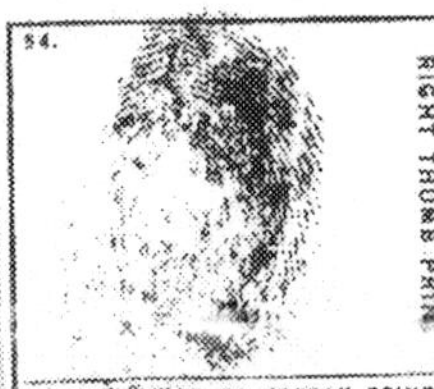

55. REMARKS (This space for completion of above items or entry of other items specified in W. D. Directives)
INACTIVE SERVICE IN ERC FROM 2 MAR 43 THRU 8 MAR 43
NO DAYS LOST UNDER AW 107
LAPEL BUTTON ISSUED
ASR (2 SEP 45) 58

56. SIGNATURE OF PERSON BEING SEPARATED	57. PERSONNEL OFFICER (Type name, grade and organization - signature)
Courtney D. Griffith	F S AUSTIN 1ST LT INF

WD AGO FORM 53-55
1 November 1944

This form supersedes all previous editions of WD AGO Forms 53 and 55 for enlisted persons entitled to an Honorable Discharge, which will not be used after receipt of this revision.

COURTNEY D GRIFFITH

To you who answered the call of your country and served in its Armed Forces to bring about the total defeat of the enemy, I extend the heartfelt thanks of a grateful Nation. As one of the Nation's finest, you undertook the most severe task one can be called upon to perform. Because you demonstrated the fortitude, resourcefulness and calm judgment necessary to carry out that task, we now look to you for leadership and example in further exalting our country in peace.

THE WHITE HOUSE

Dear - Dad & Mother

Well it is just fine I just back from eating my dinner, I had pots. gravy pie wieners & apples. I never have had my shots yet. I will get my uniform yet but I will get it this evening. They are all nice fellows my here friends & better than you could expect. You can't write me here for I think two days is all I will be here. Well I am going to write to Norma this is awful short but I do not know anything to say. so so long

Love
Dale

P.S. I'll write in the morning.

Medford Oregon
Aug. 26, 43

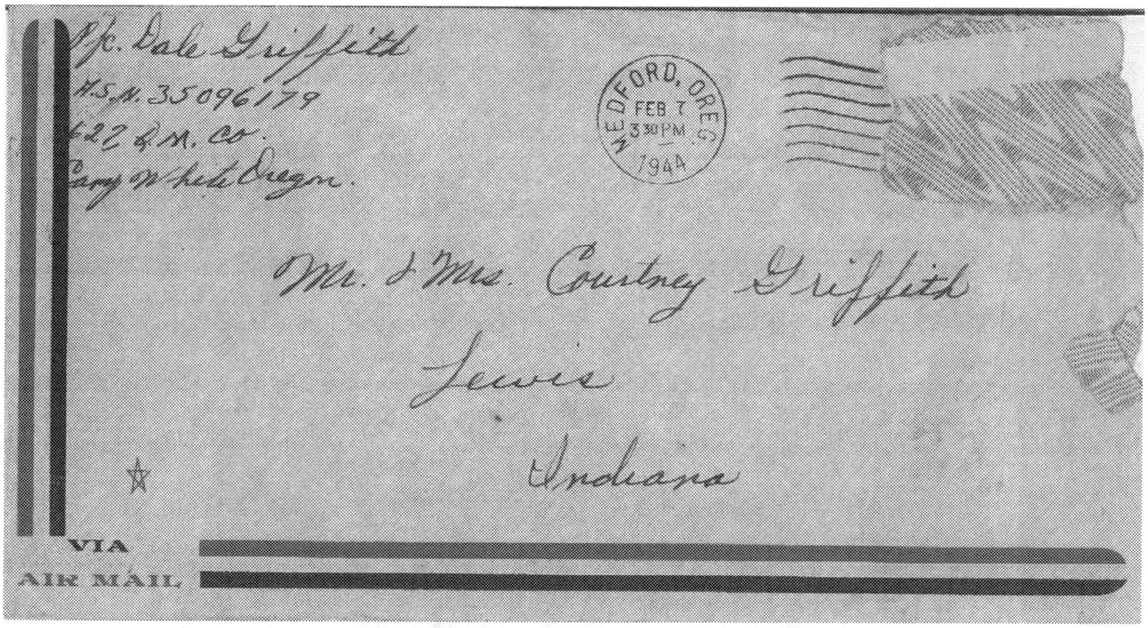
Pfc. Dale Griffith
A.S.N. 35096179
422 Q.M. Co.
Camp White Oregon.
MEDFORD, OREG.
FEB 7
3 30 PM
1944
Mr. & Mrs. Courtney Griffith
Lewis
Indiana
VIA
AIR MAIL

Printed in the United States
by Baker & Taylor Publisher Services